First published in Great Britain in 1979
by Ward Lock Limited, 116 Baker Street,
London W1M 2BB, a Pentos Company.

Printed and bound in Hong Kong.
By Book Print International
Created and produced by
Sackett & Squire Ltd.
2 Great Marlborough Street
London W.1.

ISBN 0 7063 5923 2

British Library Cataloguing in Publication Data

Best Loved HORSES OF THE WORLD

WARD LOCK LTD • LONDON

Best Loved HORSES OF THE WORLD

Peter McHoy

Contents

Introduction

Biologically, *Equus caballus* is just another species among the many thousands of animals that inhabit our planet. Yet it has achieved a unique relationship with man that sets it apart from all other animals.

Other creatures have won their way to our hearts, as any cat or dog lover will testify, and there are some wonderful relationships between dogs and men. But surely no other animal has had such a profound effect on the development of our civilization as the horse.

In most parts of the world, the horse is now used almost exclusively for pleasure, although it won our respect and affection in more austere circumstances. It was as a beast of burden and as a war-horse that this wonderful animal was first appreciated, and in that role it changed the course of history many times. It suddenly conferred great mobility and power to armed forces; the nation with the best-equipped cavalry was fairly assured of its security and victory. Unfortunately, it was on the battlefield — alongside man — that the horse suffered most, and all too frequently died.

In transportation and agriculture, the effect of the horse was no less momentous. For hundreds of years the commercial life of many countries was dependent on it. The horse worked not only on the land but beneath it too — in coal mines.

As men worked with these spendid and willing animals they became aware of the horse's undoubted charms. Even amid the seemingly cruel and harsh conditions of the mines there was usually a considerable bond of affection between the ponies and the men who worked them.

Anyone who has worked with horses is bound to feel affection for them, but there is also a particular nostalgia among most people for working horses of the past. The impact of the occasional horse-drawn dray, and the attraction of the traditional ploughing matches at rural shows, is ample evidence of this widespread love for horses.

Many of today's breeds are the result of selective breeding for specific jobs of work. The Tennessee Walking Horse was developed to walk between rows of crops without damaging them. The Hackney was selected as a carriage horse, the Shire and Suffolk as heavy draught horses, the Halfinger for its hardiness and sure-footedness in the Austrian Tyrol, and so on. All this has added tremendous variety and interest, but it is to be hoped that they will not face extinction because their specialized uses have, in many cases, become defunct. Fortunately, that gloomy future seems unlikely in view of the world-wide explosion of interest in horses, and an increased awareness of our heritage.

One breed that has an assured future is the Thoroughbred — the racehorse to beat all others. This horse exemplifies the standards that can be achieved by careful breeding. The very word *Thoroughbred* has almost become synonymous with good breeding. Indeed, many Thoroughbreds have become household names, even among people who have little knowledge of horses.

The Thoroughbreds are, of course, at the elite end of the scale, but the little Shetland ponies give no less delight to their owners. And between these extremes there must surely be a horse to suit everyone's taste.

All the many breeds mentioned and illustrated in this all-colour book have their own merits, and all bring joy to their owners. They are, in fact, the best loved horses of the world.

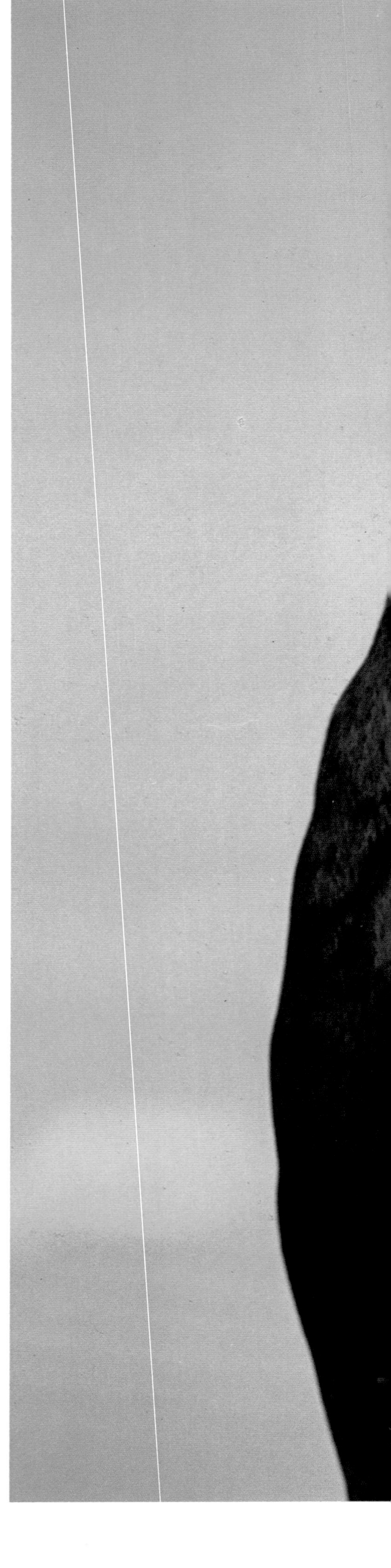

Chapter

1 Evolution of the Horse

The horse has long been a domesticated animal, and like the dog it now has a special place in our affections. It is regarded not only as a useful servant of man, but as a friend too. And the special relationship that exists between man and horse can only have been built from mutual respect and understanding, developed over the centuries as they have worked and played together.

It wasn't always like that. Only thousands of years of domestication and development have enabled us to reach this stage. In the intervening years the horse has developed into many different breeds and strains, each with its own special qualities and capabilities. The rugged little Shetland, still used in a few coal pits today, and the racing Thoroughbred have been recognized for their very different abilities, yet both are developments from a common ancestor. The Thoroughbred owes much to man's intervention, and is a superb example of how we can help nature to produce the results that we consider desirable; the Shetland, on the other hand, is an example of natural development.

Our influence on the development of the horse as a species has, however, been modest. Long before man had an opportunity to attempt controlled breeding, a considerable diversity of form had ocurred.

To put the modern horse in perspective it is necessary to look at the distant past, and fossil records provide the best means of doing this. These tell us that the genus Equus, to which modern horse belongs, was in existence a million years ago. We can in fact trace the origins of the horse back to the Eocene period, some 50 million years ago.

Left: wild horses have roamed the Kobodo district of Mongolia for thousands of years, and they still present an impressive sight — despite the fact that they were once thought to be extinct.

Above: these two foals, mutually grooming each other, are Mongolian Wild Horses, *Equus przewalskii* **a species thought extinct until Professor Przewalski discovered them alive and flourishing in the depths of Mongolia in the 1880s.**

Left: the Dulmen is one of Germany's two native ponies, and has been running in a semi-wild state since the early 14th century. Its fairly primitive ancestry can still be seen in the breed, although it has probably received infusions of foreign blood.

The evolutionary story of the horse starts in North America about 50 million years ago during the Eocene period, with fossil evidence of a small creature that has been classified as Eohippus. We also know of the existence of a European counterpart call Hyracotherium, but it is almost certainly Eohippus which provided the main evolutionary line.

These ancient 'horses' were no larger than dogs and looked rather like small deer. They had three functioning toes on the hind legs and four on the front. These animals were forest dwellers and it took perhaps another 25 million years before the evolutionary line adapted to open grassland.

During this time the key genera through which this development took place were Mesohippus, which was about the size of a sheep, Miohippus and Merychippus. All were still three-toed, but changes were taking place in the size of skull and general stature. There was a gradual increase in size, and the skull became larger with teeth more adapted for a grassland existence.

These changes were undoubtedly triggered partly by dramatic changes in climate that took place during this era. Vast plains were produced where once there had been forests. This meant not only that a change of diet was forced upon them, but they had to be able to move quickly in these open spaces if they were to avoid predators.

Merychippus was still a small animal, standing about 1 m (3 ft) high but it had a strong back and erect mane, which were a sign of things to come. It lived mainly in the eastern and western parts of North America, but some roamed as far south as the present Panama Canal and as far north as the Rockies. The creature stood on the third toe alone, being the transition to the single-toed horse that we know today.

Although various branches of the family tree had ventured into Europe and Asia, particularly the Hipparion, most became extinct and contributed nothing to the modern horse.

The animal that seems to have played the key role in continuing the line to the present day, and the direct ancestor of Equus, was Pliohippus. This single-toed animal resembled the modern horse in many respects.

Pliohippus, which lived in North America, died out, but it gave rise to Equus — a genus that includes the modern horse. Equus probably appeared about a million years ago, and at last we had a creature that was to help to feed man, to help him grow food, to fight wars, to give him sport, and to become one of the most important animals in the civilized world.

Here was a single-toed animal whose foot had the protection of a hoof and could run very swiftly; an animal with speed, strength, stamina and intelligence. And it had the robustness to tolerate quite adverse conditions of food and weather. And it could be tamed.

During the last million years the horse family, like man, extended across great areas of land, and the early horses became well established in Europe and Asia as well as South America during the Pleistocene. For some reason, however, horses became extinct in the Americas, leaving Europe and Asia as the breeding ground for future development.

Two distinct lines developed, one a large, heavily-built horse of the forests, which became extinct, and a lighter type that apparently gave rise during the last interglacial period of two famous types that bring us almost to the present day — *Equus caballus przewalskii*, the Mongolian Wild Horse, and *E. c. gmelini*, the Tarpan. These were both known to Palaeolithic hunters, who made clearly recognizable cave drawings of these early horses.

The Mongolian Wild Horse was thought to be extinct until a Russian explorer, Professor Przewalski, discovered it alive and well in the depths of Mongolia in the 1880s. It was named *Equus caballus przewalskii*, and for many years this small dun or bay coloured horse or pony was considered to be the forerunner of many of today's breeds. These ponies are believed to be one of four types to survive the last Ice Age. Its dorsal stripe and erect mane lead one to suspect the wild ass somewhere in its breeding, and this would throw doubt on the part it could have played in the development of the modern horse. Science has provided an even more compelling reason for discounting it as a forbear of the modern horse for it has a chromosome count that is different from all domestic horses; this has led to it being regarded as a distinct species, *E. przewalskii*, and it is probably best regarded as a cousin of the modern pony.

The other important wild horse is the Tarpan, the wild horse of western Russia and eastern Europe. This is a more slender horse, and likely to have had a very considerable influence on the development of the modern horse.

The Tarpan became extinct during the second half of the last century, so it may

Above: many of Britain's oldest breeds have survived on the moors and mountains, where they have been relatively unaffected by the passage of time. These mountain breeds are very hardy and often survive on a meagre diet.

Right: the Camargue, or White Horse of the Sea, is a very ancient breed, possibly a forerunner of the Barb. The semi-wild herds are a popular tourist attraction in the Camargue region of France. The dark foals are white when they mature.

Above: the Tarpan became extinct during the last century, and the specimens to be found today are 'reconstructions' of this primitive breed. Careful breeding from stock closely related to the original Tarpan made this genetic reconstruction possible.

Right: the Dartmoor is another ancient British breed, having lived on the bleak moors of this part of south-west England for thousands of years. These ponies are grazing below Hay Tor.

Left: the Shetland is another very old breed, and may have been roaming the Shetland islands, off the north coast of Scotland, for the last 10,000 years.

come as some surprise to see Tarpans alive and well today. These are in fact 'reconstructions'. They have been genetically reconstructed by careful breeding from stock closely related to the original Tarpan.

Through evolutionary forces, two distinct types of modern forerunners developed, each equipped for a different kind of climate. These are sometimes referred to as the Southern and Northern Horses, or warm and cold-blooded types. The latter terminology is confusing, for of course all horses are warm-blooded and the terms here refer to their ability to tolerate either warm or cold conditions.

The cold-blooded or Northern Horses had to survive in the colder and more variable climates of Northern Asia, and as a result had thick skins and long rough coats. The thick skin gave protection from high winds and afforded protection from the gorse and other undergrowth that they had to cope with. They probably looked rather like the Mongolian Wild horse of today, and were probably the forerunners of the heavy horses of England, Germany, Holland, France and Scandinavia.

The warm-blooded or Southern Horses, however, had a softer time, living in areas of southern Europe where the climate was less extreme. These were fine-boned animals with smooth coats. The thinner skin meant they were better able to cope with hot dry summers, but it also made them more sensitive to touch. They could run very fast, and probably gave rise to the Arab and Thoroughbred horse we know today.

Domestication

The horse has not always been domesticated. Man's first interest in the horses was as meat, and primitive men in Europe hunted them for thousands of years. At some stage it was realized that there was some merit in capturing them and keeping them for meat, milk and skins. The first tribesmen to keep small herds were probably those that roamed the plains of Central Asia.

The horses at this stage were almost certainly no more than small but tough ponies, but these early men would have realized that they could be harnessed to pull or carry loads, although they would not have had carts of course. Evidence of old writings and sculptures indicate that horses were driven long before they were ridden, and were probably used to pull a kind of slidecar or sleigh, or as pack animals.

The realization that they could be ridden was a major step forward for mankind, for this meant much greater mobility than was possible before. The herdsmen of Mongolia, Manchuria and parts of Siberia realized the importance of this.

This mobility brought about a major change in the way war was waged, and an army equipped with horses was at a tremendous advantage over those on foot. The horse has played an important part in the wars of man. At one stage they were probably bred almost solely for war purposes.

Over the centuries the horse also became used in increasingly diverse ways. Its past value on the land is obvious, but today it is the animal most linked with sports of many kinds.

The use of horses for entertainment could only come at a more developed stage of civilization, as early man would hardly have had time for such frivolities when the basic needs were for food and survival. We know, however, that the Greeks were racing horses more than 2,000 years ago.

Chapter

2 Owning a Horse

Owning a horse is a satisfying experience — but one that's bought at a substantial price, not only financially, but in time and commitment too. The decision to buy a horse should never be taken lightly or in haste. Otherwise, instead of bringing the pleasure you anticipate, it will become a burden and source of strain on both pocket and patience.

Owning a horse means that you have to be prepared to give daily care and attention, take her out, spend money on her, beautify her, be concerned for her, and above all, give her lots of your time. The rewards are great, but it does call for devotion if the novelty is not to wear thin.

Selecting the right partner is obviously important. It is not a case of taking the first one available — you need to find an animal that is compatible with you. Looks are not everything either — temperament can be as important in a horse as in a human if you are to get on well.

Anyone who's taken the trouble to get to know horses really well will understand this, of course, but it has to be said to protect horse and human from the consequences of a hasty decision.

There is nothing wrong with liking or riding horses without actually owning one. Quite often, someone who enjoys a ride at weekends at a riding school or on holidays doesn't have the time or inclination to own a horse or pony. But the pleasure they derive may be no less for that.

Left: there is something timeless about a scene like this, and it captures the whole appeal of horses. Even quite a small paddock will support a couple of horses if they are well managed.

Left: mucking out need not be an unpleasant task if done methodically and regularly. It is an essential part of maintaining a stable-kept horse.

Far left: grass-kept horses are much less demanding of time, but the grazing should be of good quality and carefully managed. Even in a small area it is worth confining the horse to one part of the grass, so that most economic use is made of the grass available.

If you are convinced that you'd like to buy a horse, you'll want to know what ownership entails — and then if you haven't been deterred, how you go about the purchase.

Money, space and time are the three major limiting factors. How much of each you have available will determine the type of horse or pony you should consider.

Some hardy ponies and horses need not be very expensive to keep, but they still cost money. No more than many other hobbies perhaps, but remember that it's not only a question of what you have available now, but what you can afford *regularly*.

It is difficult to give a firm cost of upkeep as it varies not only from one type of horse to another, but also depends on what you already have available, and where you live. What you should do is work out the costs yourself — for this is an excellent exercise not only in budgeting, but also in getting a good idea of what's involved. If you plan to have a horse or pony stabled for you, it's a simple matter of chatting to some stable owners in your area, otherwise you'll need to consider the probable cost of bedding, hay, other feeds, and rent of paddock or pasture if they are needed. Write down these headings, and detail as many costs as you can, using the information given later in this chapter as a guide.

If you live in the country you'll know where you can buy hay and probably animal feedstuffs and how much they cost but if you don't have this information, then the classified pages of your telephone directory will give you some leads. But don't overlook your local stables or riding school; remember they're buying all the requirements regularly — more importantly, they have first-hand experience and are normally run by enthusiastic people only too keen to help and advise.

When you've set down all the basic costs, remember to add a contingency fund for things like the inevitable vet's fees and rising costs. This will give you a rough idea of the running costs.

The cost of saddles and other leatherware, grooming and stable tools and equipment, blankets etc, have to be accounted for of course, but these should last some time. Remember, too, that some of these items can solve relatives' 'what to buy' problems at Christmas or birthdays!

A cost that can be avoided, but is essential if you intend to travel with your horse, is a horse-box. And it doesn't stop there — you'll need a car capable of pulling it, though often it's just a matter of a special towing bracket fixed to the family car.

Whether you attempt to stable the horse yourself will largely depend on the space you have available. It may be possible to convert some outbuilding, or you may have the room for purpose-built accommodation to be erected. It goes without saying that these are things you will have costed, organized and have ready *before* you buy your horse.

Not everyone has the resources for anything as elaborate as this of course, and often it's a matter of finding a suitable field to rent and keeping the animal out to grass. It's then a case of selecting a suitable breed, but even grass-kept horses appreciate some form of shelter, though it can be quite primitive.

Space is required not only to keep the animal, but to store all the bedding, food and tack. Needless to say it has to be somewhere dry. Remember, too, that hay and straw by its very nature is bulky, and you'll want to buy a reasonable quantity at a time to keep the cost down.

A horse or pony will demand a lot of time *regularly*. A stable-kept horse will need the most attention, a normal day starting with the first feed and mucking out at about 7.30 am, with exercise a couple of times during the day, a midday feed, and an afternoon and evening meal, as well as bed laying. Then there's grooming time on top of that. And he'll need that same attention whether it's weekend, weekday, or holiday time.

Again this can be cut down drastically by keeping a suitable animal on grass, when the amount of daily attention can be cut down.

There are other options between these two extremes, stabling the animal at night, for instance, while he has a free run during the day.

If you can share facilities with a friend this often reduces costs, and enables you to cover for each other if one has to be away.

Above: the Palomino is popularly known as the Golden Horse of the West and is surely one of our most handsome horses. It was much prized by the Spaniards in the 16th century, and is in demand today as a riding horse.

Right: the Connemara is a good all-purpose Irish riding pony. It's a tough animal able to fend for itself in poor conditions and quite suitable for outwintering.

Above: some horses, especially Thoroughbreds, have thin skin which is often made sore by stiff bridles. Nose pieces covered in sheepskin will help to prevent chaffing. Some people use these padded bridles just to give the horse a superior appearance.

Grooming

Grooming, sometimes called 'strapping', is hard work and takes a long time to do properly. Stabled horses need grooming every day, preferably more than once a day if you can. With grass-kept horses you must strike a balance between keeping the horse neat and tidy and the inevitable effects of the horse living out in the rough.

Hoofs should be cleaned out with a *hoof pick*. **Clean, healthy feet are important.**

Heavy dirt, dust and caked on mud are removed with a *dandy brush*. **This is particularly useful for horses kept outdoors. To remove dust and scurf on the body and the tail and mane, a** *body brush* **is used, in conjunction with a** *curry comb*. **The curry comb is used only to clean the body brush, which is usually done after every few strokes.**

A *water brush* **is used to wash the feet and dampen the mane. Mane combs are also used sometimes.**

Hoof oil and brush **are used to keep the hoofs in good condition.**

A linen cloth known as a *stable rubber* **is used for a final rubbing down after grooming.**

Right: never be in too much of a hurry when tacking up, and talk to your horse reassuringly. As most horses are handled from their left side, this is the best approach if you are not familiar with the horse.

Below: mounting a horse is not difficult. First, put your left foot in the left stirrup, and holding the reins and the front part of the saddle (pommel) pull yourself up and swing the right leg over the horse, gently settling yourself in the saddle.

Far right: a well-equipped rider, correctly poised on a good mount. Although proper riding clothes add to the pleasure and comfort of riding, the only really essential equipment is a riding hat and sensible shoes or boots.

Buying a horse or pony

The best advice one can give is not to be afraid to ask for and take advice. Even armed with paper knowledge it is often difficult to make a balanced and knowledgeable judgement.

It's as well to know what to look for yourself, but you may find it worth paying a vet or someone from a reputable stable to advise and give your prospective purchase an inspection. Of course, it's a matter of degree, and this becomes more important if you are buying an expensive type of horse. You may consider it less essential for a child's pony, although it's still important to match the right type of pony to the child . . . and you don't want to buy a sick animal.

You will first need to decide which type of horse or pony will best suit your needs. An established horse owner will already know the basics of choosing and buying a horse and will probably not be reading this part of the book, so it is safe to assume that this advice applies primarily to the first-time owner, who is unlikely to be buying for racing or exhibition. For most people simply want a safe and reliable horse to ride and look after, often for a child.

If you have full stabling facilities then the choice of breeds is wide open to you, but if it will be grass-kept then one of the hardy breeds will be best. Native pony breeds are usually a good choice, though many cross-breds will also do very well.

Size is not everything, for the largest horse is not necessarily the fastest; and the rider should be able to mount it easily. Sheer size does not even indicate the best weight carrier either. Even for a heavy rider, a good cob may be better than a taller hunter.

Try not to fall into the trap of overestimating your own abilities, or believe that buying a pony that's large for a child now will enable the child to 'grow into it' — it's important that they start off right together.

New Forest and Dartmoor ponies are eminently suitable for small children,

while Exmoor and Welsh ponies are better for bigger children. By the time a child reaches about 14, then anything of about 15 hands or larger can be considered. Even though it is sometimes desired to buy a pony as a surprise, always let the rider try the animal first.

Size is obviously crucial for young children, and that's one reason the Shetland is also a good choice, as they are more likely to be able to get their legs round it, which is rather important!

Don't be put off by cross-bred animals for older children. Some of the sturdier breeds are quite capable of carrying adults as well as children.

The importance of taking your time in the purchase can't be over-stressed. See as many as you feel you need to, and don't forget to ride them, and preferably tack and untack them too, to see how they handle.

You may not want to have an expert look at your selection until you've narrowed the field, but initially there are a few simple guidelines you can follow.

The animal should be well proportioned, with the legs appearing neither too long nor too short for the body; he should carry his head well, and when viewed from the front while moving the forelegs should not swing out sideways; the back feet should be lifted well. The stride should not be too short, otherwise you are likely to have an uncomfortable ride. Beware of a pony with a very short step, it could be a sign of foot trouble.

Check the feet, for it is often a point of weakness. If the foot looks unhealthy or diseased in any way, be wary. Other signs of possible trouble are the pony holding one or sometimes both front feet in the resting position; shoes worn at the toe may be another clue.

Legs are the next part of the anatomy to check, though it's fairly normal to find some minor defects, which don't usually cause problems. 'Splints' are bony enlargements that usually appear on the front legs on the bone beneath the knee. If you stand in front of the animal and run your hand down it lightly, ideally with your eyes closed, your fingers will be able to feel a slight rise or lump if a splint is present: you would be able to see a large one. Small ones should be no cause for worry.

You will also need to reassure yourself that the animal is breathing well; it should not suffer from signs of breathing difficulty after a gallop. A slight 'whistle' won't be too serious if it's just for leisure riding, but avoid one that make an excessive 'roaring' noise.

These are of course only simple broad rules, and no substitute for professional guidance.

Stables

A stabled horse spends a lot of time confined for a creature that is instinctively a herd animal of open plains. So he will need plenty of space, air, light and attention if he is not to become bored and fall victim to ill health.

His home should be 3 m x 3 m (10 ft x 10 ft) for a pony; 3.5 m x 3.5 m (12 ft x 12 ft) for a horse. The stable should have a two-part door, the lower normally being kept bolted, the top open in all but the worst weather. Horses like to be able to put a head out to see what's going on. You will find it useful to have the bolts on the bottom half free-running and loose as you often have to open these with your hands full.

The floor should be of a warm material, and non-slip, sloping towards the door to facilitate easy drainage.

Equipment should include a hook on which to hang hay nets, a manger for the food, a ring for tying him up to while mucking out, and ideally somewhere to keep tack and grooming materials and tools. Some device to prevent buckets of drinking water from being knocked over will be useful, perhaps a batten across a corner will suffice; but site it away from the food.

Bedding is generally straw, though wood shavings and sawdust can be used if these are available cheaply locally. If used together the shavings should go over the sawdust. These materials are useful if your horse tends to eat his bedding.

Straw remains the most popular material. However, some types are better than others, wheat being the best. It's also the most expensive. Oat straw has the draw-

Above and right: the blacksmith or farrier is a familiar and much respected craftsman the world over — this one is in Poland, but could just as easily be in England or America. When forges were common the horse was taken to the farrier, but now he often visits the horse.

Left: a New Forest mare suckling her foal, one of the delightful sights to welcome tourists in this part of southern England. Because these semi-wild ponies are accustomed to tourists and traffic, they are easily broken in. The stock is rounded up periodically and the surplus sold at special sales.

Far left: the German equivalent of the New Forest pony is the Dülmen, which has been known in a semi-wild state for many centuries. Like the New Forest ponies, the stock is rounded up periodically and the surplus sold.

back that some horses like to eat it — indeed it is sometimes chopped up as chaff or chop to feed to horses. Barley straw tends to be rather rough and can irritate the horse, although if it's been through a combine harvester it tends to be finer and more of the prickly awns will have been removed.

Don't be stingy with the bedding — it's false economy. If you put down insufficient, it will all become trampled and you won't be able to reuse any the next day. Pile plenty in, banking up the sides especially to make it cosy, then you'll find that a good portion of it can form the foundation for the next night.

Feeding

Hay is naturally the main bulk food, but it should be at least six months old and never mouldy or musty.

There are four main types of hay — clover, timothy, meadow and mixed. Clover is one of the best, but it needs to be of good quality. Mixed hay usually contains ryegrass, clover and trefoil, and is also good; meadow hay can be variable in quality depending largely on the type of land from which it has been cropped. Timothy hay tends to be coarse and woody.

Concentrated feeds also form an important part of a stabled horse's diet.

Oats are nutritious, but they have the effect of making the horse very lively, so be careful not give too much unless you can cope with this. They should be bruised, but not crushed too finely.

Barley is not quite as nutritious as oats. Feed it bruised or flaked, or whole kernels can be boiled. Barley is good for out-wintered horses.

Maize is sometimes fed with other grains or with cubes, especially in winter. Horses seem to like the flavour.

Bran is a useful by-product of wheat milling. It bulks out the food and tends to encourage the horse to eat more slowly and to chew more, and can be a useful laxative if fed damp. It is sometimes made into a mash.

Peas and beans should only be fed in small quantities, but can be useful for out-wintering horses, or those doing very hard work.

Linseed is said to improve coat, but do not exceed 500 g (1 lb) before cooking for a horse, half this for a small pony. A jelly is made by simmering a handful just covered with water in a pan with the lid on, which is left to cool and stand overnight. More water is added the following evening and the whole mixture brought to the boil. When cooled it should set like jelly, which can then be added to the evening feed.

Horse cubes can be very useful. They are convenient and quick to use, and contain a balanced mixture of foods with added minerals and vitamins. But of course you pay for the convenience.

Feed horse and pony cubes mixed with bran or chaff.

Gruel is made by pouring boiling water over a couple of handfuls of oatmeal in a bucket. It is fed when cool, and should be thin enough for the horse to drink.

Rootcrops such as carrots, turnips and swedes are always appreciated, but are best sliced. You can also try any spare apples.

A stabled horse should be fed early in the morning, again at noon, then in the afternoon, with a final feed at night. The last feed should include enough hay for the horse to nibble through the night if he wants. Water is just as vital as the food, and *clean* water should always be available. Try to keep it where it will not be contaminated by falling food.

Keeping a horse at grass

Even when a hardy horse is kept out at grass, some form of shelter is needed — as protection from the worst of the winter weather, and as shelter from hot sun in the summer. It also gives you somewhere to do the grooming and tacking up. It need not be an elaborate building, just three closed sides and a roof will suffice. If rugs are used, you will have to keep them on all winter.

Some concentrated feed will be beneficial at any time of the year, especially if horses are working hard, but more so during severe weather. Hay is usually appreciated during the very worst conditions when grass may not be readily available.

Do not assume that because they are getting plenty of exercise in the open field you can just turn up at the weekend and start riding them. They need to be kept in regular training if they are to give a good ride.

Management of the grass is important — if you leave a small field to a horse it will trample much of it instead of making the best use of the grass. By confining it to one third of the field at any one time, you can rest the other parts and control the grazing. An electric wire fence is a good way of keeping your horse in the right part, but avoid barbed wire.

If you notice any plants you know to be poisonous to horses, such as the yellow Ragwort, clear them — the horse will not have the natural instinct to avoid them. Needless to say, water should always be available in the field. A running stream is ideal, otherwise it's a matter of filling up buckets or a trough.

Chapter

3 Tack Talk

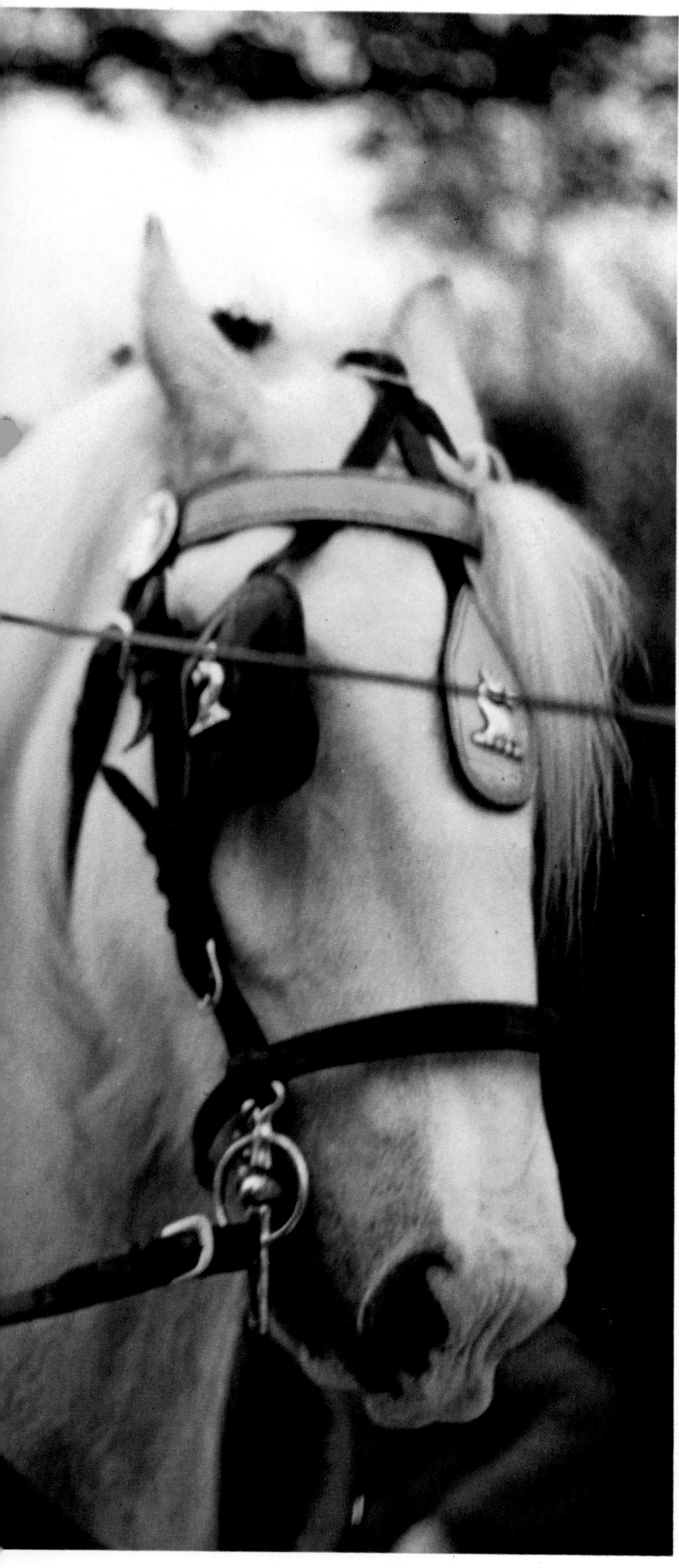

When the talk turns to snaffles, hackamores, and running martingales, blankets and bandages, tack can seem to take on a language of its own.

Tack (short for tackle) can be viewed as a mere necessity, or as an interesting and fascinating aspect of owning a horse. What you can't do is ignore it — and usually it's best to buy the best you can afford, especially when it comes to saddles.

Many centuries ago riders managed adequately without such accoutrements as saddles and stirrups — even when riding at war — but it's not to be recommended. Bits, bridles, saddles and stirrups are all very functional, and contribute much to the comfort and safety of a ride.

Over the years the basic concepts have changed little, although there have been variations. Saddles were often very ornate, with intricate leatherwork and ornamentation, and for anyone spending much of day in the saddle it could be a prized possession.

Some of the military saddles used by cavalry throughout the world were highly evolved, and had names like 'Tongs Across a Wall' and 'Extreme Fork Seat'. Fortunately the choice in your saddler's is likely to be much more straightforward, though still sometimes bewildering.

The saddle is perhaps the major piece of equipment you are likely to buy, but the right choice of bit can also be important, and even blankets and bandages can make a significant contribution to the welfare of your horse.

Left: harness horses are seldom seen nowadays, except at rallies such as the one in which these horses are taking part in Regent's Park, London. Such occasions provide the public with an opportunity to see a fine array of attractively decorated bridles and harnesses.

Below: among cultures where mass production has not removed the local traditions, some gems are to be found. These wooden stirrups are hanging on antlers of rare Andean deer at Aloa, Ecuador.

Right: this intricate-looking headpiece is a double bridle, which combines a bit known as a bridoon and a curb. It is used by experienced riders in advanced dressage and similar competition work.

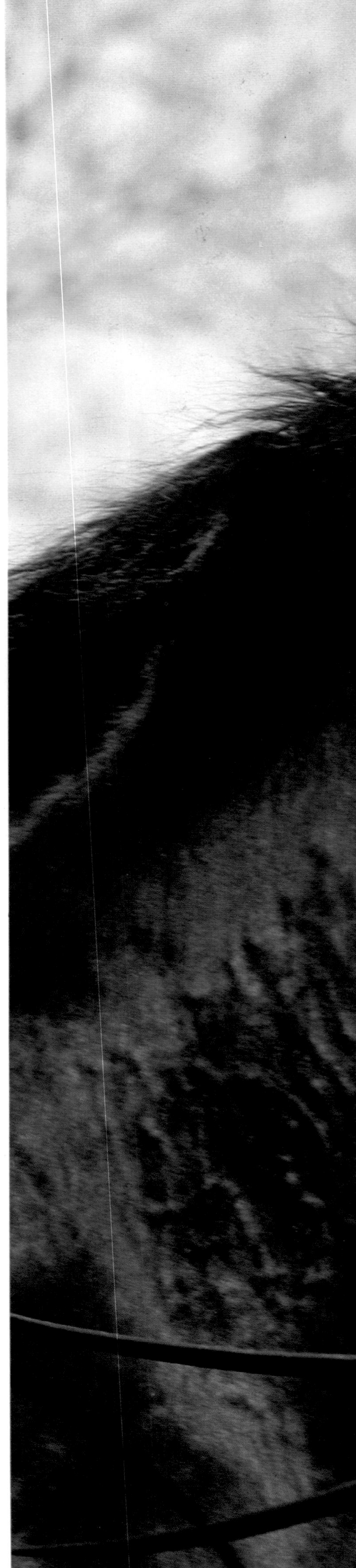

Saddles

A good saddle can be expensive, but it is a vital piece of equipment and a well-made one will last for many years if looked after properly.

A saddle should always be chosen with care, as it must be comfortable for both horse and rider. A reputable saddler will advise on the best choice within your price range — but you would do well to pay as much as you can afford.

For a beginner an ordinary straight-flapped kind is probably best, though for those who consider jumping could be their forte, one with forward flaps to encourage a position perched more forward may be best.

The width of the 'tree', that is the top bridge part, should not be too narrow for the horse, and although it should fit well down behind the withers (that's the area at the base of the neck between the shoulder blades), there should be enough space when the girths are fastened to allow air to pass along the spine, with no risk of rubbing. Leather girths are preferable to canvas.

A leather saddle should always be sponged clean after use, and not left until the next day to be cleaned. This will keep the leather in good condition.

Bits and bridles

These also come in various shapes and sizes, but most of them are designed to do a specific job. There are three principal types in use — the snaffle, the double bridle (that's a snaffle and curb bit), and the Pelham, which is a kind of double bridle.

The snaffle is the simplest and mildest form of bit, and very common. Although following a basic design there are variations in both shape and thickness of the bit. This type is often used by beginners.

The double bridle is a sophisticated type that is really a light kind of snaffle (but called a bridoon) and a curb bit. It is best used on an experienced horse in the hands of a good rider. In those circumstances it gives very good and subtle control.

Midway between these two extremes is the Pelham, which attempts to combine the snaffle and curb as one bit.

The Pelham is kind to the horse and with the right training of the rider, gives nice control without too much force.

There are, of course, other types, including the hackamore, which is a bitless bridle, the specially designed metal pieces being used to transmit the rein command as pressure on the cheeks. But for the beginner the snaffle and the

Above: the desire to decorate horses is always strong, and at shows throughout the world their owners welcome a chance to display their horses and their handiwork to an admiring public. This elaborate head-dress was pictured in Germany.

Right: these two fine horses are ploughing at a country fair in Surrey, England — and as usual on these occasions the opportunity has been taken to dress the horses handsomely.

Pelham will provide useful experience.

Be guided also by the kind of bit or bridle your horse has been accustomed to, and be especially patient during any transitional period from one to another.

The Martingale is another piece of equipment that has its place, but is unnecessary for most pleasure riding. It is useful, however, for a horse with a bad head carriage.

Bandages and Blankets

There are several types of bandage, each designed for a particular purpose.

Tail bandages afford protection while travelling, and also help to give a good line to the tail. They can be put on after grooming, but never too tightly, and should not be left on overnight.

Stable bandages are used on the legs. They are about 2.5 m (8 ft) long, and are wrapped round the leg from the knee down over the fetlock joint. They encourage circulation and keep the legs warm, but they also help to prevent injury while travelling.

Exercise bandages are about 1.8 m (6 ft) long and are used to protect the legs from injury or to support the tendons. They are applied round the cannon bone (between knee and fetlock) but not over the fetlock.

Blankets are used to provide extra warmth in the winter, and are used under rugs.

Rollers are used over rugs to keep them in place, though some rugs have their own fasteners. The roller should be padded to avoid pressure on the horse's spine.

Anti-sweat rugs are like string vests, and are used if the animal is hot after exercise.

Summer sheets are usually made of cotton, and afford some protection from flies and dust.

New Zealand rugs are waterproof and lined with wool. They are used for horses kept outdoor throughout the winter.

Day rugs are made of woollen material, and are used to keep the horse warm while standing or travelling.

Night rugs are made of jute lined with wool, and are usually used on stabled horses at night.

Chapter

4 Best Loved Breeds

Although most of us talk glibly of breeds, some of them, such as the Albino, Palomino and Cob, are really types with particular characteristics. And even those that we may think of as pure-bred often have very mixed blood, the New Forest pony being just one example.

The New Forest pony is a very old breed, living in its own part of England for many centuries, during which it was genetically 'pure'. Yet man has always found the desire to dabble with hybridization irresistible, and as far back as the 13th century Welsh ponies were probably introduced to the forest. Since then other introductions have included the Dartmoor, Exmoor, Highland and Dale, in an attempt to improve nature's efforts. Even the Clydesdale has been given its chance, and no less a person than Queen Victoria lent one of her Arab stallions to run in the forest for eight years. We still have a delightful animal, and the New Forest story is not exceptional, but it does show how inter-related some breeds have become.

Controlled breeding for improved strains is commendable, but the danger is that with native stock such as the New Forest, Connemara and Dartmoor, the true breed can be lost for ever.

The vast majority of the breeds included here have been created or improved at various times by the introduction of new blood (what better example than that most superb of horses, the Thoroughbred), and one of the fascinating aspects of our many and varied breeds is the way they relate to each other.

Left: the Norwegian Fjord pony is a beautiful creature, still showing several primitive characteristics such as the dun colouring and dark eel stripe that runs along the back. It is a strong breed and still useful as an agricultural horse in difficult areas.

Above: although called the Australian pony it is not an indigenous breed, and is a mixture of Arab, Welsh Mountain and Shetland blood, among others. It is popular as a child's riding pony in Australia.

Left: the White Horse of the Sea, or Camargue pony as it is more correctly known, is a distinctive breed inhabiting the Rhone delta, France. It manages to thrive on a diet of tough grasses and brackish water. Although the foals are dark when born, they mature into the characteristic white of the adult.

PONIES

American Shetland

The American version of the British Shetland is larger and more refined, primarily because it has been crossed with Hackney ponies. Any colour is allowed but the height limit is 11.2 hands. It is a good pet pony for a child, but the breed is also used in special trotting races.

Australian Pony

The Australian Pony is really an admixture of imported blood, as there are no truly native horses or ponies in Australia. The principal influence was the Welsh Mountain Pony, but others such as the Shetland and Timor (an Indonesian breed), and Arab and Thoroughbred horses, have also contributed.

The Australian Pony, which is hardy, free-moving and intelligent, is primarily a child's riding pony. It stands at 12-14 hands.

Basuto

The first horses to set foot in South Africa were the four landed at the Cape by the Dutch East India Company in 1653. They came from Java and were of Arab and Barb blood. These were the ancestors of the Basuto. Later other stock was imported, including Thoroughbred. The resulting Cape Horse was much used as a war horse, seeing extensive service during the Boer War. The horse found itself in Basutoland after border skirmishes, but a lack of proper care or controlled breeding led it to degenerate into the Basuto pony — a small thick-set animal of about 14 hands. The legs are short, with hard hoofs. It is also a tough, fearless animal that will gallop down terrain other horses would hesitate to tackle at a walk. They are also known for endurance — and an ability to thrive on rations that most other breeds would find impossible.

Today it has found favour as a polo pony, and is suitable for riding or pack work.

Colours are normally brown, grey, bay or chestnut.

Batak

An Indonesian pony, bred in the Batak hills of Sumatra. Arabian stock was imported to improve the quality of the native pony; these were then shipped on to other islands. They are only about 12 hands, but are quite handsome little ponies with their heads and necks showing that touch of breeding, and are quite spirited. All colours are found, including skewbalds.

Right: for many centuries wild ponies have wandered the rugged landscape of Dartmoor in south-west England. These handsome and extremely tough ponies are long-lived and make fine children's riding ponies.

Camargue
The Camargue region in the Rhone delta is the home of a very ancient breed, thought possibly to be the forerunner of the Barb. It is also known as the White Horse of the Sea, which describes both its colour (though foals are dark) and habitat. It manages to eke out an existence on tough grass and brackish water.

These semi-wild herds are a tourist attraction, but some are used for riding, and in the bullring, working the famous black bulls.

Chincoteague
The islands of Chincoteague and Assateague off the coast of Maryland and Virginia are the home of this rather rough-looking animal. How they came to be there is uncertain — some say they were originally victims of a shipwreck. Whatever the origin, they have to be good swimmers, for Assateague is uninhabited, and each July the Chincoteague ponies living there are rounded up and made to swim to the neighbouring Chincoteague, to be branded and offered for sale. Those not sold have to make the return swim the following day.

Height is about 12 hands, and many are piebald or skewbald.

Connemara
This native of the Connemara area of Ireland is a very old breed, probably descended from the Celtic pony. Not surprisingly, it is a tough animal, able to fend for itself in poor conditions. It has a number of merits, including agility, sure-footedness and a willing nature.

Although in Ireland care was taken in the earlier part of this century to keep the native animals pure, there have been additions of other blood such as Andalucian and Arab. The Connemaras are now bred in England and elsewhere.

A good all-purpose riding pony, the Connemara stands at 13-14 hands. Colours may be black, brown, bay, grey or dun.

Dale
This English breed is very similar to the Fell pony, but each has evolved slightly differently due to the habitat found on either side of the Pennine Range. The Dale comes from the Eastern side and was bred in Yorkshire, Northumberland and Co. Durham.

It is sometimes used as a trekking pony today, but it used to be regarded as a working, rather than a leisure, animal. It is a strong beast, able to carry heavy packs or pull a farm cart. For generations they were used to carry lead from mines in Durham and Northumberland to the docks, travelling about 385 km (240 miles) in a week.

The breed as we know it today contains a good measure of Welsh Cob. It stands at about 14 hands, and is often jet black, dark brown, or sometimes grey. Mane and tail tend to be long, and the feathering on the legs is considered an important quality.

Dartmoor
These ponies have roamed the bleak moors of Dartmoor in south-west England for thousands of years, which is proof enough of their hardiness. Essentially a riding pony, they are admirably suited as a child's first pony: but they are capable of carrying a considerable weight and will cope with older children — even adults — without difficulty.

At the beginning of the century Welsh, Shetland and Arab blood was introduced, though later attempts were made to minimize the damage done to the pure breed by the Shetland. It is however used as foundation stock for breeding larger cross-bred riding stock, and contributes much in this direction.

It is a sure-footed animal, sensible and amenable. It stands at about 12 hands, and the main colours are black, brown and bay, sometimes with a little white.

Dülmen
This German pony is not unlike the English New Forest pony in appearance. It probably comprises rather mixed parentage now, but it almost certainly contributed to the famous Hanoverian breed. Surplus stock of these semi-wild ponies is sold annually. It stands almost 13 hands, and black, brown or dun are the most common colours.

Exmoor
A pony of great antiquity, it is probably a descendant of one of the last of the Celtic ponies. Comparison with fossil records demonstrates quite clearly that this is a breed of exceptional evolutionary importance.

The home of this interesting pony is the wild region known as Exmoor in south-west England, where it was recorded in

Above: the Mustang, popularly known as the Wild Horse of America, was introduced by the Spanish conquistadors in the 16th century. Over the years they have bred and spread prolifically. They were popular with Indians and cowboys alike.

1085, though it was obviously roaming these moors long before that.

Bay, brown or dun are the principal colours, with a mealy muzzle and markings round the eyes. The eyes are distinctive, locally called 'toad eyes' because of their size and prominence, with the upper and lower mealy-coloured lids being prominent. The coat is also distinctive, being springy and harsh. The summer coat is close and shiny, but the virtually waterproof winter coat lacks bloom. The mane falls on both sides of the neck.

The Exmoor can be a little difficult to handle unless properly trained from an early age, but it does make a strong child's pony. They will even carry a man without difficulty. Besides those living on the moor, they are also bred in studs, and are useful in crosses with other breeds.

Falabella

This miniature horse is the smallest in the world, standing at under 7 hands. It was bred by the Falabella family in Buenos Aires in Argentina by crossing small Shetlands with a small Thoroughbred, then carefully selecting and inbreeding.

It is unsuitable for riding, but makes a fine pet, being friendly and intelligent.

Fell

Another version of the Dale, this English breed developed on the western side the Pennines, in Cumberland and Westmoreland. It is slightly smaller than the eastern counterpart, the Dale, but is still a tough animal, very sure-footed and willing. Although used as a pack pony and on farms in the past, it makes a good riding pony, and is ideal for trekking. The height is 13-14 hands, and the colour usually black, dark brown, dark bay, sometimes grey or dun.

Fjord

An attractive native of Norway, showing clear signs of its primitive origins — such as the dark stripe down the mane and back — and zebra-type markings on the legs. This strong, hardy and sure-footed

Above: the Norwegian Fjord pony is dun-coloured with a dark dorsal stripe — clear indicators of its primitive ancestry. Despite this it has probably acquired a good measure of Arab blood over the years, which helps to make it a quality breed and a good worker.

Left and above left: surely one of the most unusual breeds, the Falabella stands at under seven hands. Although quite clearly unsuitable for riding, these ponies make unusual pets, being friendly and intelligent creatures.

animal was ridden by the Vikings, and later used for light agricultural work; it is still useful in mountainous regions unsuitable for the tractor. It was also used as a pack animal, and can be used for riding or putting in harness.

Gudbrandsdal

The Gudbrandsdal originated in Norway but has spread throughout Scandinavia. It resembles the Finnish and Swedish native ponies, and like them, is a strong, hardy animal. It is used for riding and general work of light nature.

Haflinger

Originating in the Austrian Tyrol, the Haflinger is a strong, sure-footed pony suitable for draught or pack work, and being a mountain horse found much use in agricultural and forestry work in mountainous areas. It is a good riding horse for beginners, having a calm disposition.

The breed takes its name from the village of Hafling, which is now in Northern Italy; the ponies are now bred in many other countries.

Breeding in Austria is strictly controlled to maintain standards.

Highland

Like other mountain and moorland breeds in the British Isles, the Highland is a very old one. It probably descended from the primeval forest horse. Primitive markings can still be seen, including the dark eel stripe, and sometimes zebra markings on the legs. They are native to the Highland north of Scotland and to the Western Isles, where slightly different forms have evolved. Those from the islands such as Barra are smaller, standing from 12-13 hands, while the mainland type is larger and heavier, standing about 14 hands.

Almost inevitably outside blood has been introduced, mainly Arab on the Island type and including Clydesdale on the mainland.

The Highland is an immensely strong worker, and very docile. It is of course well suited to hill work, and is used by stalkers to carry dead deer over treacherous ground.

It has been used by many generations of crofters to work their smallholdings, but they are suitable for general riding.

Colours are normally black, brown, grey, bay, or dun of various shades.

Right: in their native country, Icelandic ponies used to be the main form of transport when the roads were closed by bad weather. At one time they were exported to Britain in large numbers for use as pit ponies, and used to be kept for meat production in Iceland.

Far right: the Haflinger is a beautiful pony as well as a surefooted worker in what is often difficult terrain in their native Austria. It is an excellent draught or pack animal, but equally suitable for riding.

Icelandic

The first ponies were probably taken to Iceland by settlers a thousand years ago. And as early settlers came from both Norway and the Western Isles it is believed that the Icelandic pony is a mixture of Norwegian and Irish stock of the Celtic type. Two forms evolved, one for riding and another for draught and pack work, though they could all be ridden if necessary. Until about 50 years ago in Iceland this pony was the only form of travel, especially in winter when the few roads were impassable.

The riding ponies have a fast ambling gait, which enables them to cover a good distance quickly.

Tough and sometimes independent, the Icelandic ponies have good eyesight and an interesting homing instinct; the traditional way to return a pony after a long trek was to turn it loose — it was usually back home within 24 hours.

The breed has also been used for meat production in Iceland because the poor climate was unsuitable for most other animals. These small, tough ponies of 12-13 hands were once imported into Britain in considerable numbers as pit ponies.

Kathiawari and Marwari

These two breeds are practically identical — both are Indian ponies evolved from a common stock. It is thought that their ancestors could have been a ship-load of Arab horses shipwrecked on the coast of India, which then bred with indigenous ponies after running wild in Marwar and Kathiawar.

They are rather stringy animals, narrow and lightly built, with a weak neck and quarters. Despite this characteristic they have strong legs and surprising toughness together with much stamina. They are bad-tempered animals, accustomed to living on a poor diet.

Konik

The Konik is said to be fairly recently descended from the Tarpan — the wild horse of Poland. Some of these were eventually crossed with local ponies, and the Konik is one of the resulting breeds. In fact in 1936 Professor Vetulani of Poznan University started a programme to recreate the Tarpan, using Koniks still showing primitive characteristics.

The breed stands only just over 13 hands, and is always dun in colour. It is now used to work lowland farms in Poland and other East European countries. Although local farmers do breed their own, the selective breeding is controlled by the state studs at Jezewice and Popielno.

Manipuri

This breed takes its name from that state in Assam, where it has been known for a long time. Early manuscripts suggest the breed existed in the 17th century, when it is said the king of Manipur introduced the game of polo and used them as polo ponies. Certainly they were used as polo ponies by tea planters in the 19th century.

The breed is almost certainly a descendant of the Mongolian wild horse, but it also has Arab blood. The usual height is 11-13 hands, and all colours are acceptable. It is a tough and sure-footed animal.

New Forest

As a good safe ride for children — indeed the whole family, for they are strong animals — the New Forest pony is difficult to beat. Their sure-footedness and docile, very friendly disposition, make them ideal pet ponies. The breed has been exported to a number of countries, including the United States, Canada and Australia.

Although many of these ponies are bred away from the New Forest, large numbers still live there, and sales of surplus stock occur annually. These are not as wild as one would expect and are easily broken in, for the New Forest in Hampshire, southern England, is a popular holiday tourist area, and the animals are used to people and traffic — in fact they graze undeterred along the unfenced roads. The New Forest is not in fact a forest — much of it is bare of trees and offers poor pasture consisting mainly of heather and tough grasses.

Over the years other breeds have been allowed to run with the ponies to introduce new blood, and even Queen Victoria lent an Arab stallion, Zorah, which spent eight years in the forest. As far back as the 13th century it is thought that Welsh mares were introduced. In the years since, other breeds have been tried, including Clydesdale, Dale, Dartmoor, Exmoor, Fell, Hackney and Highland.

The New Forest ponies can be any colour except piebald and skewbald, and vary from 12-14 hands.

Palomino
The beautiful Golden Horse of the West, the body a colour of newly minted gold coins, and the mane and tail almost pure white.

It is not in fact a breed, but a colour type, usually achieved by crossing two Palominos, a chestnut and albino, or a Palomino and albino.

It is known that horses of this type were highly prized in Spain at the beginning of the 16th century. There is a record of Cortez having them in Mexico in 1519, and the present name is said to come from Juan de Palomino, to whom Cortez made a gift of one.

They were popular as parade horses, and for racing until the Thoroughbred usurped him. Nowadays they are appreciated as riding horses.

Polo Pony
The polo pony is a type and not a breed — indeed the choice of breed changed somewhat when the 14.2 hands limit was abolished in 1918.

Performance is the main quality required in a polo pony. It has to be able to gallop at full speed yet stop in its own length, almost turn on the spot then gallop off again at full speed. He is often required to change leading legs at speed.

Pony of the Americas
This is a comparatively new breed, developed in America from a Shetland stallion crossed with an Appaloosa mare — the object being a dependable child's

Above: there are two Norwegian ponies — the Gudbrandsdal and the Fjord. The stockily built ponies illustrated are the Fjord type, which performs well in harness or as a pack animal, but is equally good as a riding pony.

pony suitable for the American market. They have proved themselves very worthy of these ideals, being willing and active ponies easy to ride and manage. They have also done well in jumping and trail riding.

Height is 11.2-13 hands

Riding Pony

The Riding Pony is a smaller version of the hack, and has been developed in Britain comparatively recently. The breeding stock was Polo or small Thoroughbred stallions and native mares of the Welsh and Dartmoor types. Arab blood has also been introduced.

They are aimed primarily for the show ring and there are three main height ranges — 13.3-14.2, 12.3-13.2, and up to 12.2 hands.

Shetland

Britian's smallest pony, standing at about 10 hands. It is nevertheless a tough and rugged little animal for all that. Conditions on their native Shetlands, a group of islands off the north coast of Scotland, are harsh and until the spring grass grows they sometimes have to resort to a diet of seaweed.

The Shetland is almost certainly an old breed, and has been used for centuries by the islanders as a pack animal and to haul seaweed to the land as fertilizer, and work generally on the land.

It was in the middle of the 19th century that selective breeding was attempted in response to a new market — that of pit ponies. Demand from the pits caused the breed to flourish, but today it is in demand as a riding pony, being very good for children because of its size and tractable nature. It is a lovable animal with its long mane and tail, and makes a nice pet.

The Shetland, which comes in all colours including piebald and skewbald, is now bred in a number of countries as well as mainland Britain.

Spiti and Bhutia

These two Indian ponies are similar, both being used in the Himalayan mountain regions where they carry packs or men along the perilous mountain tracks.

Both are sure-footed ponies, ideal for this terrain, and extremely hardy; they usually have to scratch an existence as best they can on the mountains. The Spiti stands at about 12 hands, the Bhutia at

Left: foals have a universal appeal, whatever the breed and wherever they are. This one is a New Forest pony in Hampshire, England.

about 13. Both can be bad-tempered, but they are energetic and hard working.

Welsh Cob

A breed of great merit, very much an all-rounder, equally happy working on a farm, being ridden, or hunting.

Its foundations probably lie with the Welsh Pony, but other old Welsh breeds probably played a significant part. They are sometimes crossed with a Thoroughbred to give increased size and speed. They were very popular with armies to increase the strength and stamina of their stock.

The Welsh Cob is 14-15 hands, and any colour can be found, although strong colours are preferred.

Welsh Mountain Pony

Another very old mountain breed, the Welsh Mountain Pony (not to be confused with the Welsh Pony, which is a larger version) is justifiably an extremely popular riding pony. Like many of the other mountain breeds it is strong, and will carry a man, but it is naturally most popular as a child's riding pony.

Over the years outside influences have been introduced. Julius Caesar founded a stud at Bala and then introduced Oriental blood. Arab blood was introduced in the 19th century, and Norfolk Roadster and Thoroughbred influences are also there. Nevertheless it still retains its distinct type, with its own definite character.

A bright and courageous breed, it has intelligence and pluck as well as endurance. It played a significant part in the make-up of the Welsh Cob, as well as contributing to the Hackney and others.

HORSES

Albino

This is a type of colouring, not a breed. Just as there are albinos in other species, they also occur in horses where a genetic fault suppresses pigmentation. The result is a white-furred animal with pink skin, and often pale eye colouring. It can happen to any breed of horse, but in America a particular strain has been evolved from a foal born in 1906 called Old King, and this is now regarded by some as a breed in its own right. The parentage of Old King is unknown, although it is thought to have been of Arab-Morgan origins.

Albinos are often used in circuses and for ceremonial occasions, and this may have given rise to the belief that they are intelligent animals. In fact there is little evidence to support this, and in some other respects, such as vision handicaps and skin sensitivity, they are really at a disadvantage.

American Quarter

This is one of America's favourite horses, and justifiably so, for it earned its place in the heart of the American people back in the days when places like Virginia were newly discovered. It was in such places that sites were cleared in what was largely untamed countryside. Horses which raced on tracks about a quarter of a mile long were called Quarter horses.

The Quarter horse was developed from Thoroughbred stallions and native mares probably descended from Spanish stock. The Thoroughbred was noted for its speed over distance, but the new breed excelled at the quarter-mile sprints.

Rapid acceleration, almost instant stopping, quick turns, and an instinctive sensitivity towards other animals, make these horses far more than mere racers. Their fast speed and nimbleness enables them to head off a steer, and their strength holds it once roped.

It is a powerful horse, with a heavy frame and strong muscles. The withers are quite low for the build, and an average stallion is usually just over 15 hands. Although chestnut is the most common colour, any solid is permissible. It has a calm temperament, making it a good horse for leisure riding, and has the merit of doing well on poor food.

American Saddle

This distinctly American horse was developed in the early pioneering days to fulfil a special need. An animal superior to the normal ranch horse was required: one to befit a gentleman and have a touch of distinction, but also good at the kind of

Above: the Palomino is a colour type not a breed, the mature pony being gold with a pure white mane and tail — a striking combination which has given rise to the popular name of Golden Horse of the West. The foal illustrated will darken with age; sometimes it takes six years to attain the true colour.

work a plantation owner might require of him. Speed wasn't as important as stamina and endurance for a whole day's ride, together with good movement to provide an easy and comfortable ride. The horse developed was originally known as the Kentucky Saddler because it was bred to work the plantations there.

A Thoroughbred called Denmark, which was foaled in 1839, is usually credited as the founding sire of the modern breed, but the Kentucky Saddler was an established line before that time. There are also traces of Morgan and other American breeds.

The result is a splendid and truly distinctive horse with a small elegant head, long fine neck, nicely sloped shoulders, and strong clean legs. To add to their appearance, the tail is carried erect by nicking the muscles of the dock and setting it with a cupper.

Today the breed is seen mainly as a show horse, competing in light harness classes or in special three-gait or five-gait classes. The horses are trained to perform one or other of these gaits: the three-gait moves at a walk, a highly collected trot with head flexed and neck and tail arched, and canter; and five-gait additionally performs a slow-gait, which is a prancing movement in slow time, and the rack, a

faster single-footed pace, each foot coming down rhythmically in a 1-2-3-4 sequence.

The normal height is 15-16 hands, and bay, brown, chestnut and black are the predominant colours.

Anglo-Arab

This is one of the most universally popular breeds, to be found in major countries throughout the world.

Clearly the influence of two pure breeds of the standing of the Arab and Thoroughbred is the reason for this popularity. It is not a true breed in the normal sense, as it is really a hybrid of the two. The definition of an Anglo-Arab varies from one country to another, although in all cases there has to be a certain percentage of Arab and Thoroughbred in its parentage.

The merging of the intelligence and stamina of the Arab with the superb performance and ability of the Thoroughbred has resulted in a very fine animal indeed. It is a horse of wide ability. It is equally happy hunting or being ridden as a hack, in dressage, in the show ring, or on the race-course.

As one would expect from a crossbreed, there are variations in physical appearance, some horses looking more Arab, others showing a Thoroughbred influence. Ideally, though, the horse should show a combination of both, with no marked bias.

Appaloosa

A distinctive breed, the Appaloosa is in much demand for circuses and parades. It is one of those breeds that once seen is never forgotten as it has unique markings. It is a spotted horse, normally having pink skin and a white silky coat, with black, sometimes chocolate, spots that can be felt with the fingertips. Other patterns are seen, including light spots on a dark background, and sometimes the typical Appaloosa markings are confined to the quarters and loins; a few are not actually spotted but have all white or marbled quarters and loins.

Although found in several countries, it is primarily an American horse — in fact its name comes from the Palouse valley in Central Idaho. The breed was developed there from stock taken to America by the 16th century conquistadors.

The Appaloosa stands at about 15 hands, and is of compact shape with strong legs and powerful quarters. An agile horse, it is fast and has stamina,

Above and left: Shetland ponies are remarkably strong for their small size, and they are very hardy. For centuries the breed has been used in the Shetland Isles off the north coast of Scotland as a pack pony or in harness. In England they were used as pit ponies.

Top left and top right: long before records were kept, the Welsh Mountain Pony was roaming the hills and mountains of its native land, where this hardy and agile breed can still be found. The breed was once used extensively as a pit pony, but happily it is now one of the most popular chidren's riding ponies.

Above: the Welsh Pony is a large version of the Welsh Mountain Pony, having had infusions of Welsh Cob and Thoroughbred blood. In most respects is closely resembles its mountain relatives.

Left: largest of the Welsh breeds is the Welsh Cob, an animal of outstanding strength and endurance. It is a renowned trotter, and an excellent riding horse suitable for riders of almost any age. The breed has a kindly nature and good weight-pulling ability, which has made it popular in harness.

while its obedient temperament makes it easily trained.

Arab

This beautiful animal is surely one of the world's greatest horses. It is one of the oldest breeds, and probably had more influence on other breeds than any other type.

Much has been written about this breed during the last 5,000 years or so of its existence. It is probably a much older breed, but there are records of actual named horses of that period. Its beauty and achievements in war have inspired artists throughout the ages.

The Arabs used to regard the best strains with something approaching idolatry. And breaking in a mare (the male was never ridden) was a ritual that was truly punishing for the horse. When she was fully developed she was mounted for the first time and ridden at full speed for about 80km (50 miles) without rest. In a state of exhaustion she was then forced into deep water and made to swim. If she did not feed freely after this ordeal she was rejected as unworthy. But the animal passing the test became a prized possession.

The speed of the Arab is legendary, and it is a horse of great stamina and staying power — also performing well under adverse and deprived conditions. These qualities did not go unnoticed or unappreciated in the Arab's native lands.

The Arab has a strong bond with humans and responds well to human companionship. It is an extremely intelligent animal, and has a perfect temperament: all qualities that endear it to the hearts of horsemen from any nation.

Ardennais

This can be regarded as a French or Belgian breed, as the Ardennes mountains from which it comes straddle both countries. This very hard horse can survive under unfavourable conditions and on far from ideal feeding, and it looks the part — stocky and sturdy, with thick neck and solid legs. It is an ideal farm horse, but was used as a cavalry horse as far back as the 16th century; they also performed well during Napoleon's campaign against the Russians in 1812. By the First World War breeding had increased the weight and size and they were used more by the artillery. The modern version stands just over 15 hands. Colours are normally bay, chestnut or roan.

Barb

The Barb is another ancient breed, originating in Algeria and Morocco, particularly the Barbary coast. Like the Arab, it has influenced many breeds, and was imported into England in large numbers in the 17th century. Today however, it is primarily a horse of North African countries. At 14-15 hands, its distinctive features are a low-set tail and sloping quarters, and rather long head. Colours are usually brown, bay, chestnut, black or grey. It is a fine riding horse, has a strong endurance, with a good turn of speed.

Boulonnais
This strong and sturdily proportioned animal resembles the Percheron in many ways, including colour — it may be dappled grey, bay, chestnut or black. It is probably a descendant of the European heavy horse, and was bred in northern France during the Crusades; Barb and Arab stallions almost certainly played a part in its development. It is strong, quick-growing and muscular, standing at 16-17 hands. They were ready for farm work at only 18 months, and in France and elsewhere older animals were used for fast coach transport before the days of railways.

Brabant
This is a Belgian Heavy Draught, originally known as the Flanders horse. A horse of great strength and sturdiness, it stands at 16-17 hands, has a short back but deep girth, and stocky legs, with feathering. Colours are normally chestnut or red roan, with some greys, bays, browns and duns.

A lively horse for its build, it is a willing worker of good temperament. The Brabant has played a significant role in the development of several other European horses, including the Ardennais, with which it was crossed to add size.

Breton
This French horse used to be bred on the somewhat indifferent land of Bretagne, which means it is a tough and hardy workhorse. Over the years, however, several versions of this breed were developed to suit different needs in other parts of the country, including a mountain version which was only just over 14 hands. The normal draught Breton stands up to 16 hands. The most common colours are blue and red roan, chestnut and bay.

Brumby
The Brumby is the wild horse of Australia, though descended from domesticated horses turned loose in the middle of the last century. They are still found in desert and mountain areas, but the Brumbies are resented by farmers who feel they graze grass needed for their own stock, and they have been culled to control numbers.

Cleveland Bay
Said to be one of the oldest established English breeds, it is a versatile horse that can be ridden, driven or used for light draught work. It has been known in the Cleveland district of Yorkshire for centuries, first used as a pack horse, and later as a carriage horse. Its smooth outline, wide deep body, muscular loins with strong quarters, and short unfeathered legs together with the bay colouring, make it a good horse to look at; this coupled with its performance, supple movement and stamina has assured its popularity as a ceremonial carriage or parade horse. It stands about 16 hands, is long-lived, and has a bright intelligence and good temperament. These qualities have made it a popular choice for mating with Thoroughbreds, producing good hunting stock.

Above: the Thoroughbred is now raced in most countries, and these fine examples are in Germany.

Right: Haflinger ponies make a splendid sight as they graze their native mountains in the Austrian Tyrol.

Left: spotted horses have always had a special attraction as circus animals. and the Appaloosa has found a ready market. Sometimes the spots are white on a dark background as this one, but a more striking version has dark spots on a white coat.

Far left: although the Arab is an old and beautiful breed in its own right, its major influence has been to improve many other breeds — a sure tribute to its merits. For thousands of years the Arabs have prized the breed and jealously guarded the purity of the stock.

Clydesdale
This famous draught horse was developed to meet the growing traffic from the coal mines and for farm work in the old Clydesdale area of Scotland. The native breed was improved by Flemish stallions imported at the beginning of the 18th century. It can be regarded as the Scottish equivalent of the Shire, though it is less hefty. Its average height is just over 16 hands. The thighs are well muscled, and the feathered legs sure-footed. The colour is normally bay, brown or black, sometimes grey, and there is usually a good proportion of white on the face and legs. It has a good disposition and in its heydey the Clydesdale was exported to many countries.

Cob
Although a type and not a pure breed, no list of famous horses would be complete without mention of it. Also known as the Riding Cob, this type of horse is often the result of chance matings as much as planned breeding. The main criteria are for a short-legged, big-bodied horse or pony that does not exceed 15.2 hands. The head should be small and set on an elegantly arched neck. The short body should be deep, and the quarters very ample. The section of leg below the knee should be extremely short. Equally important is temperament, which should be placid and good-humoured, with no suggestion of disobedience. If, in addition, the horse is able to give a smooth, comfortable ride, then you have a good Cob.

Because they are easy to mount and ride, they are especially suitable for elderly, infirm or apprehensive riders.

Danish
This small, stocky animal is a native breed of Denmark, and it is probably closely related to the Icelandic Pony. It has contributed to other Danish breeds such as the Frederiksborg.

Dutch Draught
A massive horse, standing at about 16 hands, and one of the most heavily muscled of all European breeds. It was developed after the First World War for working on both clay and sand in the agricultural areas of Holland. Stringent steps were taken to keep the line pure. No horses of unknown pedigree were incorporated in the Stud Book after 1925.

Friesian
This is a very old breed, known in Friesland in the 17th century as a desirable heavy pack-carrying horse. In the 19th century its finesse at trotting coupled with the popularity of trotting races at that time, led to the development of a lighter and faster horse, less suitable for farm work. The Friesian took on another lease of life when the problems of the Second World War made mechanized farming difficult. Breeding efforts resulted in a horse even better than before.

Because it is such a docile and willing creature, even unskilled workers could handle it on the farm. Today the same qualities and sweet nature make it popular not only as an all-round working horse but as a show horse and in circuses.

It is an animal of small stature, strong back and deep ribs. The tail is long and flowing, like the mane. The legs are feathered, sometimes up to the knee joint. Its colour is black.

Gelderland
A breed developed in the Gelderland province of Holland during the last century, the native mares of the region being covered by imported stallions such as Arabs and Norfolk Roadsters. The result was a carriage horse of some merit. Further improvements were made by introducing Oldenburg and Hackney blood, not to mention English Thoroughbreds and Holsteins. Today's Gelderland is a clean-looking horse with a stylish action that makes it a very successful show horse. It stands at 15-16 hands and is usually grey or chestnut. As well as a first-rate carriage and show horse, it also gives a good ride.

Groningen
A Dutch horse derived from Friesians and Oldenburgs, which it resembles. An attractive horse of 15-16 hands, it has a strong back, great depth of girth, refined neck and head and powerful quarters. It is at home as a carriage horse, being quick, responsive and stylish in movement, but is also used as a heavyweight saddle horse. It is an obedient and docile breed, normally in bay, dark brown, or black.

It has the merit of being an economic feeder.

Hack
As in the case of the Cob, this is not a particular breed but a type of horse with certain characteristics. The Hack is primarily a British innovation.

A Hack is essentially a refined riding horse, conforming to a standard of physique and performance. In Britain the term covers a horse or pony up to 15.3 hands, suitable for riding. The Hack should be well formed and a good specimen of its kind, but behaviour is just as important. It must have impeccable manners, walk freely, moving the shoulders rather than the head, be able to perform a collected or extended trot or canter, and stand motionless while being mounted.

In Britain Thoroughbreds usually make the best show Hacks.

Hackney Horse
A beauty to watch, the Hackney is descended from the old Norfolk Trotter, which in turn can be traced back through a Thoroughbred mating to an Arab. The Norfolk Trotter later became known as the Norfolk Roadster, and was a powerful animal capable of working on farms and elsewhere; it possessed stamina and speed. With such a background it is not surprising that the Hackney was in demand in the 19th century as a military and carriage horse.

The Hackney is more than just a practical horse — it is a beauty to watch, with its distinctive and memorable movement and grace. The shoulder action is very free and the leg is thrown well forward with a high knee ction, so that it appears to glide over the ground. The head is held high with pricked ears, and there is a general impression of alertness. All these qualities make it a favourite show horse.

The colours are usually bay, chestnut, brown or black. A typical height is about 15 hands.

Hanoverian
This famous German breed is now popular as a dressage horse and as a show jumper, but it was originally developed as an all-round horse for driving, riding and even draught work.

Its history goes back to the 17th century when local mares were crossed with Neapolitan, Spanish and Oriental stallions. Hanoverian kings of England took a special interest in the breed, and in 1735 George II opened a stud at Celle, Germany, and English Thoroughbreds were sent over to improve the breed. More recently further Thoroughbred blood was introduced, along with Trakehner breeding. Today it is a strong horse of 16-17 hands, with a bold disposition but not as fast as the Thoroughbred.

Chestnut, brown, bay or black are the most common colours, though other plain colours are permitted.

Holstein
Another German horse of long standing. Its origins are said to go back to the 13th or 14th centuries, and certainly by the 16th century it was highly regarded and exported to other countries including France. It was a heavier horse than the Hanoverian, but Spanish and Eastern influences created a lighter build, and the introduction of the Yorkshire Coach Horse into the breeding in the 19th century produced an animal well suited to light harness work or for riding. The breed was used as an artillery horse in Germany, but today it is primarily a good all-round riding horse, and a good jumper.

The colour of this strong animal, which usually stands at 15-16 hands, is normally brown, black or bay.

Although sometimes slow to mature, the breed is known for its even temper, intelligence and willingness.

Hungarian Shagya
This breed is named after an Arabian stallion called Shagya, a Syrian horse introduced to the Babolna Stud in 1836. The native stock was of dubious origins, but probably included Arab, Turkish and Persian influences. Planned inbreeding has, however, established a genetically strong line and produced a very hardy horse of 14-15 hands.

The breed has most of the qualities of the Arab, but can thrive on scanty rations. Like Shagya himself, grey is the dominant colour. It was used as a light cavalry carriage horse, but is nowadays used for riding.

Hunter
The Hunter is not a breed but a type. The best breed for a hunter must depend to a large extent on the weight to be carried,

Above: the Clydesdale is the Scottish equivalent of the English Shire, being a draught horse of similar stature. This mare has been mated with a Shire, and her foal is a half-breed.

Above left: the Camargue, also known as the White Horse of the Sea, ekes out an existence amid the tough grasses and brackish water of the Rhone delta in France. Because of their agility they are used in the bullring to work the famous black bulls of this area.

and the type of countryside over which it will have to hunt. Different conditions can call for quite different horses. The main criteria are that it should be able to give a good and safe ride, sustained for several hours over a variety of terrain. It must be able to jump clear of any obstacle.

In the show ring, much of the judging naturally has to be subjective and speculative, as hunt conditions can hardly be simulated in the ring. In some countries, such as America, the horse is required to demonstrate its jumping ability. When this is not done, the judgement has to be made partly from the experience of the judge when he rides him. In many ways the judge is on parade as much as the horse.

Some of the best Hunters are bred from Thoroughbred-Irish Draught crosses.

Irish Draught

This light draught horse is used today mainly for its ability to produce first-class hunters and show jumpers when put to Thoroughbred stallions. Its own origins are uncertain, but the Connemara was probably a predecessor.

The colour is usually grey, bay or chestnut brown. Height tends to be in the 15-17 hands range.

Lipizzaner

This is one of the world's most famous breeds, and assured a place in equine history through the marvellous performances at the Spanish Riding School in Vienna.

The breed takes its name from Lippiza in Italy, where the son of Emperor Ferdinand I, Archduke Charles, established

a stud farm in 1580. The breed was established from a cross between the Kladruber, a horse used to draw royal carriages or ridden on important occasions, and a small Italian horse with Arab blood. The breed was used in the Spanish Riding School in Vienna in 1735, when it was built for Emperor Charles VI.

The horses for the Spanish School are now bred at Piber, high in the Austrian mountains. The foals are born brown or dark grey, though most become white as they slowly mature. This can take up to 10 years. On the other hand they are often able to work into their twenties.

The Lipizzaner is a beautiful horse, shapely and elegant in appearance, with considerable presence and dignity. Their intelligent and docile nature makes them highly desirable. They also make very good carriage horses.

Missouri Fox Trotter

This unusual horse trots with its back feet but walks briskly with its forefeet. Surprisingly it gives a comfortable ride.

The breed was developed from Thoroughbred, Morgan and Arab stock, with later blood from the American Saddle Horse and Tennessee Walking Horse. It was used initially in the hills of Missouri. Height is about 16 hands, and it comes in any colour.

Morgan

This fascinating breed can be traced to one phenomenal stallion in the 18th century. It was in the 1790s, that a bay two-year-old colt was given to an innkeeper in West Springfield, Massachusetts, to clear a debt. The parentage of this colt is uncertain, but is thought to be of Thoroughbred and Arab extraction.

The innkeeper was Justin Morgan, and when he moved to Vermont, he took his horse, which he called Figure, with him. When Morgan died Figure changed hands several times, but he became known as Justin Morgan's Horse. He was given some lowly jobs to do, but not before he had established a reputation for toughness, strength and endurance — a

Above: the characteristic high-stepping, long-striding trotting action of the Hackney makes it a superb horse to watch in harness. The forelegs are thrown well forward from a high knee action, with a slight pause between each stride. The head is held high on arched neck, making this spirited horse lively and entertaining to watch.

Above right: although the Irish Draught was developed primarily as a farm horse, these natural jumpers often produce excellent hunters and show jumpers when mated to Thoroughbreds. When this horse was used in the First World War, heavy losses were suffered and later the breed became so depleted that export restrictions were imposed.

reputation that was spread far and wide.

He was a horse of 14-15 hands, but with very considerable strength for his size, excelling in weight-pulling contests as well as performing well in harness and timber-pulling. He was also raced but was never beaten.

Justin Morgan's horse was also put to stud many times, and he seemed to be able to produce foals with an astonishing uniformity — his offspring showing the same kind of qualities.

Justin Morgan's horse was eventually bought for a substantial sum by the US Army, and the Morgan Stud Farm was established. His progeny served in the cavalry, the police and fire service, as well as in a variety of other useful roles. He died in 1821 at the ripe age of 32.

This truly remarkable horse also contributed to other famous American horses such as the Standard Bred, Tennessee Walking Horse, and the American Saddle Horse.

The normal colours are bay, brown, black and chestnut, and a typical specimen stands at 15 hands. Today it is used as an all-round leisure horse, being versatile and possessing a very good nature. It is happy under harness or saddle.

Mustang

Another legendary American horse, sometimes called the Wild Horse of America, although it is not truly wild — the Mustang is domesticated quite easily once caught.

These symbols of the Wild West are descendants of the horses introduced by the Spanish conquistadors in the 16th century.

Other Spanish horses were introduced later, and it was inevitable that some of these horses would escape and run wild, or be captured by Indians. Over the years the Mustang has bred and spread prolifically, and was an attraction for early settlers and Indians alike. The Indians bred a particular version called the Indian Pony, and the white man managed to tame them and work them as cow ponies.

All colours are found in this hardy animal, which stands at 14-15 hands.

Oldenburg

The Oldenburg is a German horse that has changed its form somewhat over time, to adapt to changing needs. It was known in the 17th century, and its early use was as a carriage horse. It was not, however, very robust and hardy. Barb, Spanish and Neapolitan Blood was introduced, and later further improvement was attempted with Thoroughbred, Norman, Cleveland, and Hanoverian crosses. The result is a large saddle-horse of 16-17 hands.

Orlov

Count Alexius Orlov was a man of considerable power and property, not to mention action (he conspired to murder Czar Peter III). One of his milder pastimes was breeding horses, and in the latter half of the 18th century succeeded in producing one of the finest trotters. He started with an Arab stallion and a Dutch mare. Gradually English Thoroughbred, Danish and Mecklenburg blood was introduced, and a superior trotter was the outcome. These met the considerable demand for trotters in Russia.

It is a strong, powerful horse, standing at about 16 hands. Grey and black are the most common colours.

Percheron

This heavyweight French draught horse has a beauty and elegance of movement that has helped to make it popular in many countries beyond its native France.

It originated in the Perche region of France, probably as a development from the working horses of northern France and Belgium. The Percheron is a surprisingly active animal for its size, which usually approaches 17 hands. Unlike the Shires and Clydesdales, the legs are clean, without feathering.

Pinto

The Pinto is not a breed, although horses with the correct markings are now considered to be a breed in America.

The name Pinto comes from a Spanish word meaning painted, and some do indeed look as though they have been painted.

The colouring can be either piebald — that is broken patches of black and white — or skewbald — patches of white and a colour other than black. There are two recognized types of pattern: the Tobiana and Overo.

The Tobiana describes a white coat with dark markings, the Overo has a dark coat with white patches. Tobiana horses tend to be larger than the Overos.

Because the broken coat was regarded as good camouflage, it was a favourite with the Indians as a war horse. The breed is popular today in both Canada and America as a riding horse.

Polish Arab

The Polish people have always been well-known as horse lovers, and Arabian horses have been bred in Poland since the 16th century. The Polish cavalry of the 17th century was a formidable opponent.

The Arabian horses were first captured during the many wars with the Tartars and Turks, and studs have been established for many centuries, the oldest being the Slawuta Stud, formed in 1506.

In 1803 a horse-buying expedition was sent to Arabia, and it has been a mark of Polish policy to introduce fresh blood into

Below: Lipizzaner horses are world famous for their performances at the Spanish Riding School in Vienna. This picture was taken at the Szilvasvarad stud in Hungary, and shows the superb conditions under which these fine horses are stabled.

Right: a once familiar sight on the farms of Europe — French Percherons ploughing. Although replaced by the tractor, they still manage to put in an appearance at ploughing matches, specially dressed for the occasion. The Percheron was exported to many parts of the world.

the local stock. The Polish Arab stock has been exported and has played an important part in the breeding of Arabs in other countries.

Rhineland Heavy Draught
This German heavy draught horse, sometimes known as the Rhenish, was developed during the heyday of the draught horse. It is a bulky, powerfully built horse, deep and broad. It matures early and is said to have a good temperament. It stands at 16-17 hands.

Schleswig
In the Middle Ages the Schleswig was much used to carry heavily armoured knights, and centuries later was in demand for coping with heavy loads of another kind — hauling trams and buses.

Today's horse is compact in form, standing at 15-16 hands; the dominant colour is chestnut, but greys and bays also occur.

Shire
England's most famous agricultural horse, and one of the largest in the world, it stands at 17 hands, weighs a tonne and is capable of hauling five tonnes.

Its origins lie in the heavy horses of Medieval times, referred to by historians as the Great Horse of England. It probably descended through the Old English Black Horse. Despite its size it is a remarkably mild animal, being gentle and docile. It matures quickly and can be worked on farms at three years, which also made them attractive commercially. Although bred mainly in the agricultural shires of Lincoln, Cambridge and Huntingdon, where for centuries it has been popular on the land, it was for generations an equally familiar sight in city streets, and is still used occasionally to pull brewers' drays.

Standardbred
This famous American trotting horse is a superb animal — being a good racer whether trotting or pacing (moving legs laterally instead of diagonally). Those animals which show a natural tendency to pace while young are specially trained to develop this gait.

It looks rather like a more robustly built Thoroughbred, an ancestor that was crossed with a pacer of Dutch origins. The Morgan also played a part.

This most popular horse for trotting races stands at 15-16 hands, and main colours are bay, brown, chestnut and black.

Suffolk
Like the Shire, this is another much-favoured English draught horse, and a distinctive one at that. Unlike the Shire it has clean legs, like the Percheron, and is always chestnut in colour, although the exact shade may vary.

The breed, which comes from the Suffolk area of eastern England, was mentioned in records going back to the beginning of the 16th century, and the modern version can be traced back to a foal born in 1760.

The Suffolk stands at about 16 hands and weights about a tonne, but it is very active and can be worked from a two-

10

Above: another popular English heavy horse — the Suffolk Punch. This old breed, known in the eastern countries for centuries, is strong and powerful, but unlike the Shire or Clydesdale is quite capable of an impressive trot.

Left: perhaps the most famous English draught horse is the Shire — in height and weight it is certainly the greatest. Yet despite the sheer size of these horses they are docile and easily managed. These two are ploughing in a match at Windsor, England.

year-old until its mid-twenties. It is mild and docile in temperament, and can thrive on quite meagre rations. It also tends to live to a good age.

Swedish Ardennes

This has been the most popular heavy draught horse in Sweden, and was developed from the Belgian Ardennes imported in 1837, although other blood was introduced later. These horses are energetic but good-natured, and stand at 15-16 hands. Predominant colours are black, chestnut, bay and brown.

Tennessee Walking Horse

An American breed, the Tennessee Walking Horse was developed to suit the needs of plantation owners and farmers who wanted a horse that would walk easily between the rows without damaging crops.

As with the Morgan, the breed can be traced back to one proginator — Black Allan, a Standardbred trotting stallion foaled in 1886. Black Allan showed a marked preference for moving with a peculiar gait half way between a walk and a run — now a characteristic of the breed. It makes for a good ride — claimed to be one of the best in the world.

The merits of Black Allen were fortunately realized and he spent many years at stud. He sired many horses in his time with the same characteristics as himself, and a uniform breed was established.

Colours are usually black, bay or chestnut, and they stand about 15 hands. Besides his half run, half walk gait, he

Right: the Thoroughbred is synonymous with excellence the world over, and strains have been established wherever horses are raced. All Thoroughbreds can be traced to three Arabian sires — Darley Arabian, Godolphin Arabian and Byerley Turk, mated to English mares.

Far right: a German breed of outstanding merit, the Trakehner at one time contributed much to the power of the German cavalry. Today it is happily put to more pleasant tasks as a show jumper or saddle horse, and many international awards have been won.

walks normally, canters, and trots well in harness. A general-purpose horse of good disposition, it can be used for agricultural work between the shafts, as well as for fine riding.

Thoroughbred

The Thoroughbred is the horse at its peak of perfection. A picture of grace and elegance and a wonderful racing machine that has no equal among horses.

All Thoroughbreds can be traced back to three famous Arabian sires — Byerley Turk, Darley Arabian, and Godolphin Arabian. They were crossed with English mares, though whether these were pure native stock or already had some Eastern blood in them is not clear.

The Byerley Turk was brought back to England by Captain Robert Byerley, who had captured it from the Turks at the seige of Buda. It was this horse that led to the Herod line of Thoroughbred racehorses. Herod, sired by Byerley Turk's grandson Tartar, sired winners of £200,000 prize money, a phenomenal sum in those days. Many of today's famous racehorses are his descendants.

In 1704 the Darley Arabian was imported by a Yorkshire squire named Richard Darley — and it was one of the strains most prized by the Arabs. His descendants not only include the never-beaten Eclipse but over a hundred winners of the English Derby.

Last of the three founding fathers was the Godolphin Arabian. There are various stories describing how he was discovered. He came via Paris and some say he was found pulling a cart in the streets of that city. He was purchased by Edwin Coke and later bought by the Second Earl of Godolphin. This horse went on to establish the Matchem line, and his progeny won £151,000 in prize money.

By the last quarter of the 18th century the Thoroughbred breed had established itself and did not depend any longer on imported Arabian stock.

By 1730 an Eastern type stallion, who was a son of Darley Arabian, arrived in the United States. By the end of the century other famous English stallions had been imported, and the principal blood-lines of today were established.

Australia received its first Thoroughbred at stud in 1799, and English imports together with Eastern stallions that arrived via India had established the Australian Thoroughbred in the first quarter of the 19th century.

New Zealand has also produced many famous Thoroughbreds, and now all major racing countries of the world breed and race these fine animals. In some cases, slightly different strains have developed in various countries, but they all have the classic line and performance of the English Thoroughbred. And like the Arab, they have influenced many other breeds in the course of their history.

The colour of the Thoroughbred is usually brown, bay or chestnut, although they can be any solid colour. The average height is about 16 hands, but can vary between 14 and 17.

Trakehner

Perhaps the best German breed, the Trakehner was originally known as the East Prussian Horse. It was developed at the stud of Trakehnen, founded in 1732 by King Friedrich Wilhelm I, father of Frederick the Great. At the beginning of the 19th century however, Arab blood was introduced, and later Thoroughbreds played a very important role in the composition of the modern Trakehner.

It was primarily used for the German Army, being an excellent cavalry mount.

When the Germans retreated from Poland at the end of the Second World War, less than a twentieth of the 25,000 registered horses made the three-month trek from East Prussia (now part of Poland) to what is now West Germany.

The Trakehner stands at about 16 hands, can be any solid colour, and possesses considerable stamina as well as a good temperament. It is a first-class saddle horse, and a good show jumper.

Waler

This is an Australian horse, the name Waler being taken from New South Wales, which is where the first horses were introduced into that country.

The first horses to arrive came from the Cape and from Chile in 1795, the foundation stock being of Dutch and Spanish origins. But these were small horses and the settlers needed better mounts for riding the vast lands, so both Thoroughbred and pure Arab stock were introduced as improvements. An admixture of these breeds produced the Waler, which is a fine horse with perhaps more stamina than the Thoroughbred, and a good disposition.

During the gold rush days of the 1850s, stock tended to be neglected and deteriorated badly; fortunately, some of the new-found rich began to take an interest in horses and racing, and the breed was steered towards its former standards, and improvements made.

Chapter

5 Horses at Work

The horse has served man in many ways, and shared in his pleasure and pain. The same animal that is the source of so much pleasure and sport also fought alongside man in many bitter wars. In peace it has served him faithfully, keeping the wheels of commerce and agriculture turning for many centuries.

It is sad that the animal that has brought so much benefit to mankind should also be used as a vehicle of war. Yet that was probably one of its first uses, and until the beginning of the 20th century they were as important to any army as the weapons with which they fought. Thankfully the military horse today is hardly likely to be subjected to anything more rigorous than the parade ground on ceremonial occasions.

For thousands of years man has also used the horse to oversee his livestock. And the rancher still uses it today, having tried motor vehicles, helicopters and hovercraft. A horse can move amongst the cattle in a way mechanized transport cannot. And it's possible to survey stock from the saddle in a way which is not possible from the seat of a Landrover.

Although today it is easy to look with disdain at the slow pace of horse travel, the impact of the improved communications it made possible in its day were as far-reaching then as the jet engine is today, if not more so.

Left: although harness horses are now used almost exclusively for ceremonial occasions or display, it was not always so. Horses like these fine Arabs worked hard to speed man comfortably on his way.

Above: there is something almost timeless about a scene like this, but when horses are one's business, as at the Savar stud in Hungary, it makes sense to use them in traditional ways.

Horse-drawn transport

For thousands of years the pack horse, carrying its load in panniers, was the principal means of carrying goods. Over very rough and inhospitable country, especially in mountainous areas, the pack horse still has advantages over modern transport.

Wheeled transport, at first in the form of primitive carts, opened up the possibility of increased loads and speeds. Horses have been used to pull carriages and wagons for thousands of years (in fact Tutankhamen had a state chariot 3,000 years ago), but it was the coming of the stagecoach that brought the biggest social change.

The forerunner of the stagecoach was the stage wagon — the predecessor of all public vehicles. During the opening years of the 16th century these creaking wagons made their way slowly and tediously through the countryside. They were used by the poor who could not afford their own mount. By the end of the 16th century goods became a regular aspect of road-haulage.

The goods wagons were drawn by perhaps eight horses, and these had to be supplemented by another two, sometimes four, more on some of the hills.

The stage-coach, drawn by four fast horses, carried the wealthy inside, the poor outside, and the very poor in a basket at the back!

Life for the stage horse was hard — cruel by today's standards. In the early 18th century coaches had the same horses for the whole journey, which meant slow and tiring progress. When flying stages were introduced, where horses were changed every 24 km (15 miles) or so, speeds increased.

But it was still punishing work. Horses were treated so brutally, three years was their maximum working life. Eventually, with better planning and more understanding, the expected working period was increased to seven years on slow coaches, but was still only four on the fast ones. The expression 'to die in harness' was not without meaning then — in 1821 it happed to 20 horses on one mail coach route alone. But to keep up appearances, the best horses would be used during daylight hours and the sick ones at night!

It was a natural progression from the stage-coach to the horse-drawn omnibus and tram, and equally inevitable that both should succumb to progress. But for many centuries the horse was the prime mover of goods and people, both within and between towns. Their impact on forming the towns and societies we know today should never be forgotten.

No mention of horses in transport would be complete without acknowledgement to the largely unseen work of those ponies that hauled their burdens under extremely unpleasant conditions — the pit ponies. At the turn of the century there were over 70,000 of them at work in Britain's mines, and surprisingly a handful are still employed today.

These ponies had to be small to work within the confined spaces, and usually

Right: in the rural areas of some countries one man and his horse still cultivate the soil in age-old fashion — often with quite impressive results. This picture was taken in Spain.

Shetland, Fell and Welsh breeds were used. They lived underground hauling trucks of coal on rails from about the age of four years until they were too old to work. They were, nevertheless, well cared for with affection by the men who worked them.

During the 19th century the horse became the main motive power for another important form of transport — the barge.

Canal and river barges were often laboriously poled along or hauled by tough men, often of an unsavoury kind. The idea of using horses for this work had been considered before, but until towpaths were provided, the horse could not be used.

In Britain it wasn't until the beginning of the 19th century that towpaths were constructed, but they soon spread, and the tranquil scenes of horse-drawn barges became an everyday sight.

On the rivers where larger boats could ply their trade, several horses were used to haul a boat, but canal barges were almost always handled by a single horse. In fact there was often sufficient power in hand to tack another barge behind. The exception would the passenger barges, or 'package boats' as they were called, which were normally handled by two horses — one hauling from a bow rope and the other from a stern rope. A postilion usually rode on the second horse.

Life for the barge horse was not too harsh, and the greatest physical effort came in starting from a narrow lock. The horses had to be specially trained to 'hang in the collar' to get things moving smoothly. To help ease the barge along on the right course, the rope was passed through special pullies to a fixing on the fore of the lock — this gave a kind of 'double pull'. Once the barge was moving and the bow was level with the fixing, the transition was made to direct haulage.

Young or untrained horses were usually blindfolded before tackling long aquaducts or tunnels, which could be alarming for a novice horse.

It was only a matter of time before mechanization made the towpaths redundant except as convenient places for fishermen to sit.

The draught horse that worked the canals also provided stirling service in the city streets, where they kept everything from coal to beer on the move. As with the barge horses, animals of the stature of the Shire and Pecheron were used to haul these heavy loads, and they were the backbone of commercial traffic for centuries.

Above: In the mountain regions of Austria and elsewhere, traditional forms of transport are not much use, but specially designed sleighs serve admirably even in these treacherous conditions. The first horse-drawn vehicles were probably a form of slide-cart.

Right: A complete contrast from the Austrian mountain scene, yet the horse is still there serving man regardless of climate or conditions. This picture was taken in Fez, Morocco, and shows not only a different lifestyle but the unusual saddles and stirrups used there.

Above: rare scenes like this almost make one willing to relinquish the convenience of the motor car. These two Arab horses appear to be aware of their breeding and beauty.

Left: a stockman can move on horseback among his sheep or cattle in a way that would be impossible with mechanized transport. This Gaucho is herding sheep in Rio Grande do Sul, Brazil.

Previous page: horse taxis still ply for trade in Afghanistan, adding colour to the sun-drenched streets.

On the land

Some horses such as the Mustang, the wild horse of the West, seem to have an instinctive way with cattle, and are able to move easily amongst them.

In many ways the cow pony has to be rather like a polo pony — quick, alert, intelligent, able to change direction and speed almost instantly, and possess a great deal of courage.

As any cowboy film fan will know the West was won on horseback, and the relationship between stockman and horse has to be one of understanding when the whole day can be spent in the saddle.

Even today, whenever sheep or cattle are kept on a large scale or on wild terrain, the rancher's horse is still to be found in numbers — in America, Australia and New Zealand. In Australia several hundred horses may be kept on a ranch; they would have been Walers in the past, but today the are just as likely to be Thoroughbred.

In America, too, the Mustangs have given way to horses of more refined breeding, such as the American Quarter Horse. This horse became a firm favourite with the stockmen because of it nimbleness and fast starting and sprinting which enables it to head off a beast quickly. Its sturdy build is also useful when strength is needed for roping steer.

On the smaller, British type of livestock farm and arable farms where the terrain is less rugged, the working horse is sadly a nostalgic memory of the past, but for many centuries the horses that pulled farm carts and ploughs improved the efficiency of the agricultural economy.

Breeds that provided some of the finest heavy horses at the plough, often in pairs, were in many cases descendents of those originally used to carry knights in armour — strong, hefty animals with plenty of power. In Europe especially, breeds such as the Percheron, Breton, Shire, Suffolk Punch and Clydesdale were popular with farmers and public alike.

There would be hot debate about the relative merits of the breeds — whether for instance the clean-legged types such as the Suffolk Punch or Percheron were superior to those with feathering round the legs such as the Clydesdale and Shire.

Horses at war

The horse in active service came to a dramatic close with the last major cavalry charge at Musino, near Moscow, during the Second World War. In less than 15 minutes, 2,000 Russian mounted soldiers

Below: from early times the horse has helped man to fight his wars — suffering and dying alongside his master — for the mounted soldier was at a great advantage over adversaries on foot. The formidable-looking character here is taking part in a film in Samarkand, USSR.

Right: the Life Guards, seen here in The Mall during a Trooping of the Colour ceremony, are one of the tourist attractions of London. These highly trained and extremely well-matched horses make a marvellous spectacle with the colourful uniforms of the guards.

were killed. The number of horses killed must have been equally great.

However, it was the horse that changed the course of history on many occasions, for the army with the best cavalry was at a considerable advantage over foot soldiers, to whom the sight and sound of a charging horse must have been a quite terrifying experience.

The Assyrians are believed to have had mounted bowmen about 900BC, and the fact that they needed both hands to use their bows demonstrates that the horses must have been well trained. The Assyrians also used chariots, which in turn were copied by Persian, Egyptian, Greek and Roman armies. The chariots could be terrifying, and sometimes contained six warriors — two drivers, two bowmen and two soldiers holding shields. The horse could also be used to transport supplies.

The chariot fell out of use however, except for hunting and racing, and the cavalry became the front-line troops.

The Roman horses had to be strong as the cavalry wore armour and carried a spear, short sword and shield. Riding must have been difficult as the Romans did not use saddles or stirrups and had to keep their seat by gripping the horse with their thighs.

The Tartars, fierce horsemen riding Mongolian ponies, were the first to use saddles with stirrups and snaffle bridles. In the 13th century they conquered land from the Baltic to the China Sea.

Eventually it became clear that horses could be used very effectively to haul guns to the battlefield. The type of horse used varied not only with the period and place, but with the type of artillery. Heavy cart-horses were needed for the heavy field batteries, but for light artillery guns strong riding horses had the advantage of being able to go into battle at a gallop.

War created a formidable demand for horses. Even in 1918, when a fair amount of transport had been mechanized, there were probably over 70,000 horses or mules involved in transportation from base or rail-head. Then there were the horses allocated to fighting units. And with heavy casualties it is easy to see why private and many trade horses were commandeered, and large numbers of horses shipped from places like Canada and Argentina.

The sight of horses in gas masks at work in the most atrocious conditions for their masters, and sometimes suffering terrible injuries, is surely the best but tragic example of horse in the service of man.

Chapter 6 Horses for Pleasure

Whenever people have had leisure, they have not been slow to realize the value of the horse. Roman soldiers knew the thrill of racing chariots when they had a little spare time, and today's trotting races are the modern version of chariot races. A surprising number of our equestrian sports have their origins in the military field.

The principles of classical riding and dressage were laid down with preparation for war in mind. A cavalryman's life was at risk unless his horse could be perfectly controlled with one hand, and was able to change step and position as well as manoeuvre smoothly with the minimum of control.

Eventing is another legacy from the military schools, the courses being designed to test whether a charger would be able to cope with the demands of long distance riding at a fair speed, travelling over open country and taking any obstacle in its stride. Such courses are testing for the rider too, for apart from a lot of exhausting riding he must be able to pace the horse so that it does not become over-tired and unable to complete the next task.

Of all sports, however, it is racing that must take pride of place. Whole towns, such as Newmarket in England, can be taken over by the breeding, training and racing of horses. Millions of pounds each year are waged on horses. The 'form' of each one is studied by a special breed of men who spend their lives assessing the quality of horses. At big races whole nations become involved in the tense, final moments of the race, and some famous race horses, such as Red Rum, become household names even among those who would never place a bet, let alone go to a race-course.

Left: horse racing is largely a spectator sport, but more and more people are enjoying the thrill of racing in the saddle. This race at Heathfield, Sussex, England, is for ladies only, although sometimes men and women do compete in the same races.

9
2

Above: man's ingenuity is never found wanting when it comes to sport, and this is one way of making the most of a cold climate. The specially designed racing sleighs are ideal for this kind of harness racing.

Left: in some countries racing would be called off in conditions like these, but in places such as Switzerland both horses and riders learn to cope with them. This race is taking place at St. Moritz.

Dressage

Dressage is, at its best, like a ballet for horses. It presents a real test of horsemanship, showing the worth of horse, trainer and rider alike.

It was only in the 18th century that dressage entered our equestrine vocabulary, but the origins of this classical horsemanship go back much further — as far as the Greeks in fact. They studied and worked their horses for the pleasure of seeing accomplishment while at the same time improving the standards of the cavalry horse.

Dressage has been in and out of vogue through the centuries of course, though usually it seems to have survived in the more advanced civilizations and societies. It was revived after the Dark and Middle Ages in Renaissance Italy, and in the late 17th century began to take the form in which we know it today.

Some of the finest examples have been encapsulated in the classical schools of Austria and France. Perhaps the most famous of all is the Spanish Riding School in Vienna. Here the white Lipizzaner horses perform the same kinds of steps and movements as their predecessors some 400 years ago.

These famous horses have great strength yet are light and graceful in action and show a considerable aptitude for this kind of display work. They originally came from Spain — the result of Arab and Barb stallions crossed with native mares. Although they come in various colours only the white ones are used by the Spanish School. Although they leave their mothers at six months old, the real schooling doesn't begin until they are over three, when they are broken in; and it's another year before they are trained seriously.

The steps and movements seen at the Spanish Riding School shows what can be achieved, given the right combination of horse, rider and time.

The Lipizzaner is first ridden for less than an hour a day while being trained. This is when the horse first learns the rider's signals, or aids as they are also known. Lessons become more difficult as they have to learn smooth changes of pace, harder turns and sideways movements.

Only the best horses are able to perform 'airs above the ground', and these are not part of normal dressage. As the name implies these are spectacular leaps

Right: trotting is a popular sport in some countries, where the breeding and training of trotting horses is becoming an important business. The sport is the modern equivalent of chariot racing.

Far right: point-to-point races were originally run to please riders rather than spectators, and were quite literally run from one point to another, with little regard for the audience. Nowadays the courses are planned to give the spectators a good view of the race — this one is at Heathfield in Sussex, England.

and jumps. It may not be obvious at first that even these movements served a very useful purpose at war, but by leaping away from the enemy, or raising his front legs, the horse could save his rider's life.

It is really only in the 20th century that dressage has become a spectator sport. Before that it was generally practised only in military establishments or the riding schools maintained by royal courts. The future of this refined level of riding was more or less guaranteed by the inclusions of dressage in the Olympic programme of the Stockholm Games of 1912.

The field is open today to almost anyone who feels they have the time and ability to reach a reasonable standard. There are widely recognized grades and usually competitions for some of them at most shows. Each grade has its own set of movements to be performed, and naturally the more advanced the grade, the more difficult the work to be done. Only at advanced levels would flying changes of legs and pirouettes be included.

The pirouette is an example of the suppleness and responsiveness that can be achieved during a dressage performance. The horse has to turn a complete circle on the spot, keeping all four feet moving in a canter sequence. The front legs step in a circle round the back ones, which remain almost on the same spot.

Another advanced movement is the Piaffe, which tests balance, strength and control. It is really a slow trot on the spot, the horse springing alternately from one front and back leg to the other.

Certain breeds have a reputation for being most suited to dressage, the Lipizzaner being an obvious example. Other breeds popular for this kind of work are the Hanoverian, Holstein and Trakehner, though other breeds are used, often with much success.

Show jumping

Watching a horse jump seems so natural nowadays that one wonders why it took thousands of years of horse riding before people realized the thrill and excitement of the sport. The answer lies in the fact that there just wasn't much need to jump. Even in war, the most horses were likely to be asked to cope with would be the occasional ditch or small bank. It was only during the 18th century when land owners in Britain began to enclose their fields with hedges and fences that it became clear one could not adequately cross the countryside without jumping. Of course, once it became a necessity on a wide scale, the thrill of jumping did not go unnoticed.

Its natural evolution was steeplechasing, which is discussed on page 87, and it took perhaps another hundred years to move from steeplechasing to show jumping. It seems to have been in the 1860s that riders began to jump their horses at shows; the 1866 Harness Show in Paris was a notable one. Here, however, the riders only paraded in front of the ring to show their horses to the public, then departed into nearby countryside to jump natural obstacles. Obviously this wasn't all that exciting for the spectators, and soon the idea of bringing fences into the arena seemed to make more sense.

It was natural that in England jumping should form part of the agricultural shows, and it is known that this was taking place in London in 1876. By 1900 'lepping' competitions, as they were known, were to be found at all the major shows. But the emphasis was placed on style. This gave the judges plenty of scope for political awards, and often confused competitors and spectators alike. This led to the formation of the British Show Jumping Association, which set about standardizing rules. Throughout the world it is now a well-organized sport with clear sets of rules, though these obviously vary to some extent from one country to another.

In the United States of America the National Horse Show took place in New York for the first time in 1883, and by the early years of this century the sport had become well established throughout many parts of the world.

The first International Horse Show was held at Olympia in London in 1907. By 1912 jumping was included in the Equestrian events of the Olympic Games.

There is no 'standard' course, and much is left to the individual designer, but normally it is between 457 m (500 yd) and 823 m (900 yd) long and includes between 10 and 16 fences. The fences are supposed to be as natural as possible. The height of each fence may very, but they should never be so difficult that no horse achieves a clear round.

There are two principal types of fence — the straight fence and the spead fence,

Below: bullfighting is an emotive sport, but the qualities required of the horse are not disputed. It is necessary to twist and turn with considerable agility, and be able to gallop fast with rapid acceleration. In many ways it requires the characteristics of a polo pony.

Right: there are three main types of circus act using horses — bareback riders, riderless horses demonstrating skill and obedience, and acts which demonstrate the virtuosity of a single horse and rider. These solo performances demand considerable skill and expertise.

the latter calls for a jump with width as well as height. The straight fence includes gates, planks, stone walls, posts and rail, and brush and rail (the lower half being brushwood). Spread fences, introduce a horizontal dimension, having further posts, bars or obstacles a short distance from the first.

The Double-oxer has bars either side of a brush, while a Reverse Oxer has bars with brush either side; the Hog's Back has three sets of bars, the centre set being higher than those either side. The water jump is another obvious example of a spread fence.

With the exception of banks, the horse is expected to make a single jump or effort.

An important part of the fence is the 'ground line', for this is what the horse uses as his cue for jumping. A wall comes down to the ground, giving a clear line, but a single bar some distance off the ground has no clear ground line, and this makes it very difficult to jump. The same fence with a bar added at ground level becomes very much easier. For novices a loose pole is usually laid down to give a line on fences that do not have a natural one.

Combination fences, that is several fences following each other closely, add spectator interest, and test the suppleness of the horse. The sequence is usually regarded as one obstacle. A narrow style-type jump is another test of the horse's obedience. For height-jumping ability the high wall provides the test.

The basic rules for fences is that if any part of it is knocked down or lowered (including flags, shrubs or other accessories) it is counted as down even if part of it is arrested in its fall. On the other hand, if a lower bar falls but the top one remains in place, there is no penalty. If there are several parts to one jump, no extra faults will be incurred even if more than one part is knocked down.

Points can also be lost through what are termed 'disobediences', and include a rectified error, where the horse takes a wrong course and has to be corrected by the rider. A refusal is when the horse stops in front of a fence, though if he doesn't knock it down, and doesn't rein back but immediately makes a standing jump, all is well. If, during a refusal, a fence is knocked down, the clock is stopped while it is rebuilt, and various time penalties incurred. If the rider is unfortunate enough to be dismounted, he has to remount before the clock is stopped. If a horse avoids an obstacle or jumps it outside the flags he is said to have run-out,

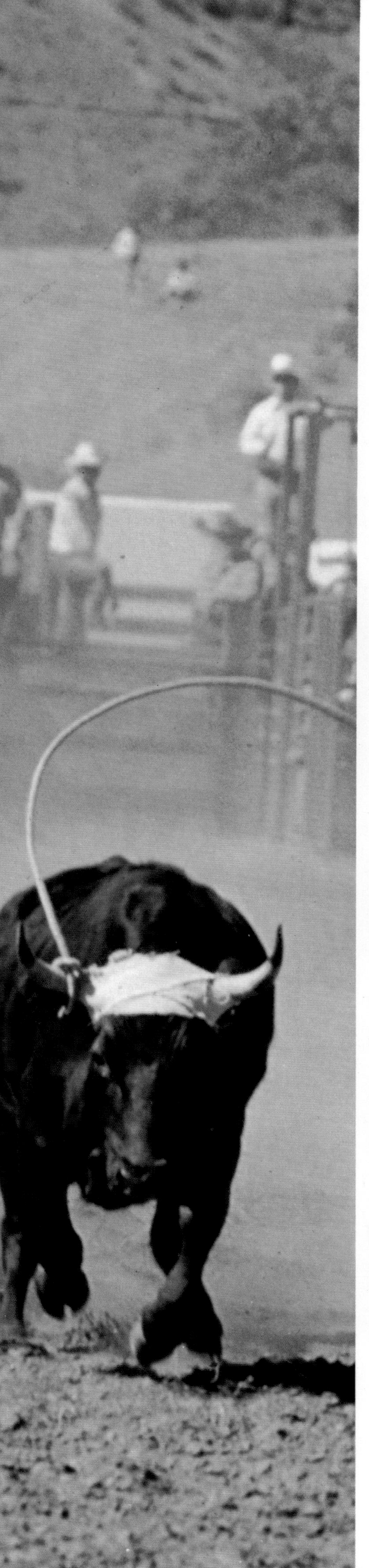

and must return to retake the jump or be disqualified. Another possible fault is resistance, which is when the horse stops, refuses to go forward, reins back, turns round, or shows some other disobedience.

Knocking down a flag at a compulsory turning point will not be penalized.

The time element ensures an interesting competition. A course will have a 'time allowed', within which the course must be completed to avoid incurring a penalty, and a time limit (double the time allowed), beyond which the horse is eliminated.

There is much more to any set of rules of course, but for the beginner these should give an idea of what to look for and add to the enjoyment of watching what has become a very popular spectator sport in recent years.

Eventing

Eventing, by which is usually meant a three-day event (though it is compressed into a two-day or even one-day event for less experienced riders), is one of the toughest tests a horse and rider can face. It calls for skills in many areas, quite apart from outstanding physical stamina on the part of both mount and rider.

The basic eventing tests were devised as cavalry training. The early military tests concentrated on cross-country work and obstacles, with a fast steeplechase section, but later a dressage test was added to demonstrate control. The jumping test was to prove the animal capable of further work at the end of the more physical parts of the course.

The three-day event has followed this pattern very closely, and the competitors face the same kind of difficulties.

Day One is set aside for dressage. This calls for special control and restraint on the part of the horse, as he is likely to be very fit and ready for the racing ahead. In the dressage arena he has to execute slow and exact steps, as well as demonstrate obedience. A supple and calm horse that moves smoothly and rhythmically under command is required. The

Left: steer roping is a popular Western sport packed full of action. It is exciting to watch as it demands a well-trained horse and considerable ability to handle a lasso. The horse is trained to step back to keep the rope taught as soon as the calf has been lassoed.

Above: horse and rider are put to the test at a bucking bronc sale in Miles City, Montana, in the United States. Bronc riding is another popular and fast-moving rodeo sport, and one which calls for both skill and courage on the part of the rider, as it is a dangerous sport.

rider's carriage and the way he gives directions to the horse are also under scrutiny.

Day Two sees the speed and endurance tests, of which there are four parts. The first and third is over roads and tracks totalling 10-20 km (6-12 miles), which are ridden at a slow canter or trot. The second phase is a steeplechase course of about 2-4 km (1-2½ miles) which will need to be taken at the gallop, and finally there is the cross-country course of 5-8 km (3-5 miles) with a variety of obstacles, again ridden at the gallop.

Between each stage the horses are examined by a vet, to ensure that they have not been overtaxed and are fit enough to tackle the next stage.

Day Three sees the final test of jumping a course of 700-900 m (750-1,000 yd) with 10-12 obstacles.

The open country parts of the course can vary considerably from one meeting to another, but this is intentional, for horse and rider must be able to cope first time riding over unknown territory and unexpected hazards. However, the rider is allowed to walk the course before riding.

Racing

Horse racing is very much a spectator sport, but to the riders, trainers and owners involved it is a serious business, and whole industries are based on it.

There's nothing new about racing horses. The ancient Greeks were known to practise the sport over 2,500 years ago. Subsequently, chariot racing was popular and racing in one form or another has been with us ever since. We know racing was popular in Roman Britain, and in the early part of the 16th century there are records of races being held at York and Chester in England.

Racing has been called the sport of kings, and certainly it developed apace in England with a Royal following. Queen Elizabeth I is supposed to have gone racing at Salisbury in the year her navy were victorious over the Spanish Armada, and James I created Newmarket, one the world's most famous centres.

Above: dressage competitions demonstrate the degree of understanding and control that can be achieved between rider and horse. Modern dressage is a legacy from the military schools, where fine control of the horse was taught as a matter of survival.

Left: pony trekking is becoming a popular holiday pastime in many countries, offering novice and expert alike a chance to explore the countryside at a leisurely pace from the back of a pony. These young riders are near Dolgellau in Wales.

Charles II owned and bred some of the best horses of his day, and also had a significant influence on Newmarket.

Queen Anne was responsible for building Ascot Racecourse in Berkshire, England, where one of the world's most famous race meeting — the Royal Ascot — is held each June.

Despite Royal patronage, there were some pretty corrupt practises in the early days of organized racing, but about 1750 the Jockey Club was formed. This body removed the rackets from English racing and laid down sets of rules to improve standards and laid the foundations of racing as we know it today.

A major milestone in the organization of races was the introduction of a handicapping system. The first major handicap race was the Oatlands Stakes in 1791, when extra weights were imposed to equal the chances of all the horses, ranging from 57 kg (126 lb) to 33 kg (73 lb). Handicapping increased public interest because it tended to make betting more interesting.

At the turn of the century in America racing was banned in many states because of corrupt practices — despite the establishment of a Jockey Club in 1894. Only a couple of states escaped, including Kentucky, and even here the authorities had to ban bookmakers shortly before the 1908 Kentucky Derby. But without betting to attract the crowds it seemed almost impossible to make racing a success.

A solution was imported from France — what was in fact a totalizator system, where the odds and dividends were decided in direct relationship to the money staked on each horse. It was an instant success, and the totalizator system is a popular method of betting today in many countries. It also provides a good way of collecting levies and taxes, as a percentage of the total staked is deducted before dividends are calculated.

Now the United States holds a leading position in the world of horse racing.

Most racing in the world is flat racing, and in countries like America it operates the whole year round; in Europe however, the flat season runs from March to early November, with the National Hunt season filling in the gap. Steeplechases are run on at least a 3-km (2-mile) course which includes hurdles or fences of birch or gorse. Although steeplechasing takes place in other countries, it is a distinctly English sport, having its origins in the hunt. As the name implies, the original races were run from one village steeple to another. The first traceable record of a steeplechase was in 1752 when a race was run in Ireland from Buttevant Church to the spire of St Leger Church, a distance of 4½ miles (about 7.2km). The name St Leger has been given to one of the famous English races.

Point-to-point is another type of race that had its origins in the hunt. In fact, while steeplechasing was being organized on more official lines, the hunts carried on with their cross-country races, quite literally from one point to another. Amateurs took part, but it wasn't considered a spectator sport.

Gradually spectators were considered more and the course planned to come back to finish at the starting point. Nowadays courses are usually sited where spectators can park their cars at a vantage point to watch the day's racing.

The horse that has undoubtedly had the most profound effect on racing is the Thoroughbred, which is the race horse *par excellence*. The development of this superb horse is described on page 62.

Trotting

Trotting is descended from the ancient sport of chariot racing, and in many countries horses are bred and trained specially for this type of racing.

There are two types of trotter, each being trained to move in a different way. The true trotter uses a diagonal action of near fore and off hind alternating with off fore and near hind; the Pacer moves laterally using near fore and near hind and then off fore and hind.

The horses run round special tracks pulling a light carriage designed for racing. If the horse breaks into a canter during the race he is eliminated.

Endurance riding

A much more recent sport is endurance or long distance riding, which although now established in the United States and Australia, is still quite a newcomer to Britain. It is a strenuous test for the horse, advanced courses being up to 160 km (100 miles) in a day in Britain, though some are only half this. In other countries the distances vary but they are all in this range. However, novices are not expected to tackle this kind of distance, and such rides are for the experienced. Pleasure rides of 24-48 km (15-30 miles) are best to start with. Only later do riders enter the competitive field with trail rides of 40-96 km (25-60 miles) in the case of Britain, though in countries like America the distances can be greater, spread over more tha[illegible]ne day.

[illegible]ant part of endurance riding [illegible]ary checks, which are made [illegible]ges, for the horse should [illegible]ondition.

[illegible]ractions of this sport is that [illegible]breeds, and is suitable for any age of rider. Children sometimes accompany adults on the shorter courses.

Holiday hacking and trekking

Trekking is becoming an important tourist attraction and holidays with horses are available in many countries. The essence of these holidays is to enjoy the quiet and beauty of the countryside from the vantage point of the back of a horse or pony, and to enjoy the thrill and closeness with horses that comes from leisurely riding.

The beauty of these holidays is the relaxed pace — trekking involves travelling at a walk; if you want something faster then you need a hacking holiday, where larger horses are used for more conventional riding. Either way it is wrong to start off with a competitive spirit or a hurried manner. Remember that if you are in a group, many of the members, especially if you are trekking, will be beginners.

If *you* are a beginner, check before you go that tuition is available, and that you can borrow suitable clothing, such as a

Above: eventing is a tough sport, where, as part of the test, rider and horse are expected to tackle an almost unknown course and to cope with a variety of obstacles. The horse needs to have complete confidence in his rider in eventing of this kind.

Above right: polocrosse is a popular Australian sport, a hybrid between polo and lacrosse. The modern game had its origins in England, although a similar game was probably played in Japan a thousand years ago.

Previous page: polo is a taxing game for the tough polo ponies, which have to be very agile and able to change pace and direction quickly and without hesitation.

riding hat, if you do not have your own. And whether you are used to riding or not, do take sensible clothing. Beachwear can look attractive but it's hardly practical for this kind of holiday. Even if you've been used to an hour or two's riding in reasonable conditions, you may be surprised how cold and miserable you can feel if the weather turns cold and wet when you're several hours from base.

Hunting

It is ironic that in its early history the horse was itself hunted for food, and now is used as a hunter of the fox or other quarry.

Hunting for pleasure is primarily of English and Irish origin, organized hunts being known 300 years ago. Now, of course, there are hunts in many other countries throughout the world, but its stronghold is in Britain.

Hunting provides interesting and varied training for both rider and horse, as well as the very considerable excitement and atmosphere of the chase itself. There is also the very special pageantry that goes with a meet, and the unique relationship of the hunt and the country scene.

In Britain the fox is the traditional quarry, but in France deer, hare and wild bore are still hunted. At first Australian hunters contented themselves with kangaroos and other native animals, but later imported the fox. In America both the native grey fox and the imported red versions are hunted.

Foxhunting has also played a significant part in the improvement of breeds. In the days of hunting boars and stags, the horse had to possess the stamina to last long days hunting in the forests, but there was no requirement to have the ability to jump hurdles at speed. It was only when man began to hunt the fox in more open countryside that speed and jumping ability became of prime importance.

A number of different breeds are used in hunting, but one of the most popular is a cross between the Irish Draught and the Thoroughbred. In fact many hunters are cross-breds. The result has been a constant upgrading of the hunter in all its forms, and that has been of value to the horse world generally.

Polo

Polo is an ancient game, and one of the oldest horse sports, originating more than 2,000 years ago in Persia, although it was also known throughout the East. It was introduced to England via the Indian continent, where the game was especially popular with Maharajas and army officers. It was being played by tea planters in Assam in 1850, and it had found its way to England by 1869. It was a group of army officers who first demonstrated the game on Hounslow Heath, outside London. In those days the game was played with eight riders.

The game has changed little over the years, the modern rules being aimed primarily at safety. The number of players on each side has, however, decreased to four, which is due primarily to the increase in the size of the mounts. The small Manipuri ponies used in Assam were only about 12 hands high, whereas the modern 'pony' (often they are small horses) is just over 15 hands, though they can be taller. The modern polo pony is also faster.

A polo pony is a special animal — tough, fast, alert, and very agile. It has to be able to stop in its own length from a full gallop; flying changes of leg must be routine; and it needs a strong back and quarters.

Quick stops and 180 degrees turns are essential moves, which means the animal is subject to many strains and stresses. The legs particularly are subject to stress, and supporting bandages are always worn; the mouth too can suffer from the sudden checks of the rein.

In addition the animal must respond easily and quickly to instructions, and be ridden with one hand only.

The most famous polo ponies come from Argentina, where the game is very popular, and the native ponies are rugged animals well suited to the rigours of the game.

Although the game can be quite difficult for the spectator to follow because of the small size of the ball, which is only 83 mm ($3\frac{1}{4}$ in) across, and the speed of the game, the rules are quite simple. The game is divided into periods of play, each called a chukka, which in Europe lasts for seven minutes.

There are six chukkas, though the number varies in different regions. There is a three-minute break before each chukka, with five minutes at half time. More than one pony is needed as no pony is allowed to play more than two chukkas.

One of the four players initiates the attack, backed up by two of his colleages, while the fourth player acts mainly as defence. The object is to get the ball through the opponent's goal, and each time one is scored the teams change ends. There is an handicapping system so that in effect the better players have goals deducted. Other rules are concerned mainly with safety and regulating who has right of ball in various situations.

Above: the water jump is always an exciting one to watch, and at international courses like this one at Hickstead, England, they pose a difficult test even for experienced horses. Here Hartwig Steenken is on Erle.

Left: an experienced rider like Caroline Bradley can make a jump like this look easy, but jumping of this standard comes only from years of training — and, of course, a good horse.

The ball is usually made of ash, willow, or bamboo root. The polo stick or mallet is normally made of cane, ash or sycamore, with a right-angled head for hitting the ball.

Polocrosse

Polocrosse is particularly popular in Australia, and is a hybrid of polo and mounted lacrosse. A polo-type stick is used with a net on the end instead of a mallet head, and a soft ball is used. A team consists of three players.

Although the modern version has its origins in England, a similar game was probably played in Japan a thousand years ago. It was never popular in England, much to the relief of polo enthusiasts who thought it would take support from their game, but it has become very popular in Australia.

The rodeo

For lots of action in a short space of time, the rodeo takes some beating. As one would expect of a sport with its origins in ranching, it is primarily an American and Australian pursuit, but the daring of bareback bronco riders is known and admired the world over.

Rodeos are a legacy from the pioneering days of the Wild West, when, after work was done, cowboys would brag about their prowess at breaking in a horse or roping a steer in record time. Naturally some were required to put their boasts to the test, and that was the beginning of rodeo shows.

Several mounted sports can be seen at a rodeo but the most famous is bronc riding.

Bronc riding is a short but spectacular event — in the case of a saddled bronc the rider is expected to remain on his horse for only 10 seconds, eight in the case of an unsaddled animal. That's no mean achievement when an unbroken horse is bucking and kicking violently. To encourage them to react violently a belt is placed round the animal's body and tightened just in front of its hind legs. This makes the horse buck more furiously.

The rules are simple; the rider has to remain on the horse for the minimum specified time, using only one hand and holding the other above shoulder level (if he touches the horse with it at any time he is disqualified). To make the event more difficult the rider is expected to jab the horse above the shoulder with his blunt spurs as the horse is released. The judges award marks for the horse's performance as well as the rider's, to even out any anomalies that might occur from one contestant having drawn a livelier horse than another.

DeReszke
FILTERS
CUT THE COST
— OF SMOKING
CHINA CUT CAFE

Without doubt bronc riding must be one of the most action-packed spectator sports.

Another rodeo event that clearly reflects the skills of the ranchers is steer roping. It is based on the cowboy's skill rounding up and catching calves for branding.

This is a straight race against time. Once the calf is released from its pen the competitor rides out with the lasso in one hand and a piece of rope in his mouth for tying the animal. The calf is lassoed and almost at the same time the other end is tied round the special horn on a Western saddle, while the horse must stop immediately the calf is lassoed. The competitor leaps from his horse, which pulls back to keep the rope taught, and turns the calf over. He has to tie three legs together with the rope he has between his teeth, then raise his hand in the air. It is sometimes possible to do all this in less than 15 seconds! If however the tying has been done too hastily and the calf gets a leg free within five seconds the competitor is disqualified.

Another somewhat hair-raising spectacle is steer wrestling, or bulldogging as it is sometimes called. Once the steer has been released at the start the rider gallops level, another cowboy riding on the opposite side of the animal to keep it running in a straight line. When he is level with the steer the rider throws himself on it, grabbing the horns and digging his heels into the earth to bring the animal on to its side.

There are other traditional horseback rodeo events such as racing round barrels, trick and demonstration riding. At the larger shows it is possible to see colourful horse-drawn wagons.

Rodeo sports are exciting but often dangerous. Less hazardous are events where Western-style riding is demonstrated. This involves holding the rein in one hand and sitting with straight legs slightly forward in the stirrups. Such shows also provide an opportunity to dress in traditional Western costume.

The main features are stock seat riding and classes for stock, trail and pleasure horses.

The circus horse

Although the circus ring may seem far removed from the more traditional arena, many acts demonstrate extremely skilful training and riding. In the 19th century, one trainer could get his horses to perform so well that military instructors became his pupils; yet another circus rider became an instructor at a cavalry school.

There are three basic types of circus act involving horses. 'Liberty' horses usually perform in groups, without riders, following the instructions of their trainer. The second type is usually performed by a single horse or in a small group, demonstrating advanced movements and steps on the lines of dressage. Thirdly, there are the bareback riders who use strong stocky horses, sometimes called Rosinbacks because resin is rubbed into their backs to ensure a firm footing for the riders. Smoothness of movement and good balance are required from both horse and rider.

Left: the Tenby Hunt meets in a town square in Wales — a sight guaranteed to collect a crowd of onlookers. The barking of excited hounds and the horn call of the master all make the start of a hunt an exciting occasion, and for the hunters a moment of anticipation.

Above: once in open country the real hunt begins. This one is in Sussex, southern England, and fox will be the quarry. Although fox hunting has many opponents, the sight and sound of a hunt in full cry is a thrilling experience that most people find memorable.

Index

Page numbers in italics refer to illustrations

Acknowledgements

The publishers would like to thank the following photographic agencies for their kind permission to reproduce photographs in this book:
Bruce Coleman Limited: 4/5, 6/7, 8/9, 11 (top), 12 (bottom left), 14 (bottom left), 15 (top), 16/17, 20 (bottom right), 22 (top right), 24 (bottom left), 24/25, 26, 27 (top left), 28/29, 30 (top left), 30/31, 33, 37 (top), 38 (top right), 39 (top), 40 (top), 40 (bottom), 41 (top), 42 (top right), 44 (top), 45 (top left), 46 (top), 47 (top left), 47 (bottom left), 48 (top left), 48 (bottom), 48/49, (top), 49 (top right), 50 (bottom left), 50/51, 52, 53 (top left), 55 (top), 56 (top), 58 (middle), 58/59, 61 (top), 62 (top right), 63, 66 (top), 74 (top left), 76/77, 81, 82 (top left), 84/85, 85 (middle), 87 (top left), 91 (top), 92, 93 (top), 94/95, 95 (bottom right).
Zefa Picture Library (U.K.) Limited: End papers, 10, 12/13, 14 (top), 18, 19 (top left), 20 (top), 22 (bottom right), 23 (top), 32 (top), 34/35, 36, 43, 54 (top), 57 (top), 60, 64/65, 67, 68, 68/69, 70/71, 72, 73, 74/75, 78, 79 (top), 80 (top right), 82/83, 86 (top), 88/89, 90 (top).

Front cover: Zefa Picture Library (U.K.) Limited
Back cover: Bruce Coleman Limited